25 YEARS INSIDE UNIVERSAL STUDIOS

From Tour Guide to
Entertainment Director

JERRY GREEN

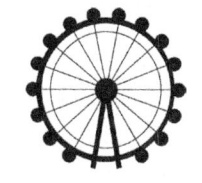

Theme Park Press
www.ThemeParkPress.com

© 2017 Jerry Green

No part of this publication may be reproduced, distributed, or transmitted in any form or by any means, including photocopying, recording, or other electronic or mechanical methods, without the prior written permission of the publisher, except for brief quotations embodied in critical reviews and certain other noncommercial uses permitted by copyright law.

Although every precaution has been taken to verify the accuracy of the information contained herein, no responsibility is assumed for any errors or omissions, and no liability is assumed for damages that may result from the use of this information.

Theme Park Press is not associated with Universal Studios, nor its partners or affiliates.

The views expressed in this book are those of the author and do not necessarily reflect the views of Theme Park Press.

Theme Park Press publishes its books in a variety of print and electronic formats. Some content that appears in one format may not appear in another.

Editor: Bob McLain
Layout: Artisanal Text

ISBN 978-1-68390-057-3
Printed in the United States of America

Theme Park Press | www.ThemeParkPress.com
Address queries to bob@themeparkpress.com

CONTENTS

Introduction v

Opening Scene *1*

The 1960s *7*

The 1970s *41*

The 1980s *91*

The 1990s *149*

It's a Wrap *167*

About the Author 171

*More Books from
Theme Park Press 173*

OPENING SCENE

I boarded a plane at Sky Harbor International Airport in Phoenix; destination, Hollywood, California.

To most people that doesn't sound like a big deal, but California, show biz, actors, and Hollywood seemed completely out of the reach to a poor kid born in a small town in North Florida. And when I say *poor*, I'm not speaking of a state of mind, but of finances. My family was poor.

I was the youngest of four kids—two sisters and a brother—and although we grew up poor, we learned to make do and live on what we had. I remember more than once coming home and finding bags of groceries on our front porch, left there by local churches.

We lived in an old rundown house, which fortunately had a couple of acres of land in the back. So, my dad decided to raise hogs. He started with a few, but the number increased to forty or more, all sizes. Forty pigs might not sound like a lot, but to us it was. I remember one of the hogs was really mean and enjoyed chasing my brother out of the pen when he had the chance. He was tasty.

But the pigs came with a lot of work, primarily for my dad and brother since I was only five. Some mornings I would wake up at 3:30 a.m. to go with my dad and brother to restaurants and collect "slop" (leftover food from the night before). The restaurants dumped the scraps into large drums that we collected every couple of nights and took home to feed the hogs. One of my favorite stops, which was only once or twice a week, was the bakery. After getting home we picked out the items that looked edible and kept those for ourselves. The hogs got the rest.

I once went with my dad to the slaughter house to sell some of our pigs—that was quite the experience for a five-year-old. We also had chickens, a cow, and of course what every five-year-old boy should have, a pet goat. Yes, rather than a dog, I had a goat named Billy, which I cleverly shortened to Bill. We wrestled and played just like any boy-dog relationship. Bill was rarely tied to a stake, and seldom penned up. He had the run of the property. He did everything a dog does and more, including keeping the grass manicured to an acceptable level, and eating everything left unattended.

My dad altered a red wagon by removing the handle and replacing it with shafts, turning my Radio Flyer toy wagon into a buggy. Then he fashioned a harness to fit Bill. It was like a horse and buggy from the Old West. Bill and I won first place in Panama City's Fourth of July parade. The grand prize was a blue ribbon, and Bill's and my picture in the local newspaper.

The family cow, and my goat, presented a special challenge for my mom. She had to go to the back of the pasture to milk the cow. As she returned to the house, Bill would follow, butting her in the backside causing the milk to slosh out of the pail. Getting back with half a pail of milk was considered a victory. She and Bill enjoyed a love-hate relationship. He loved to chase and butt her, and she hated running the gauntlet after milking the cow.

When I was about four, my dad, my brother Wayne, and I were run over by a dump truck. My dad was badly crippled, my brother was also severely injured, and me ... I was hit and knocked across a ditch into a rose bush filled with thorns. However, to hear my mom recount the story, I wasn't technically in the accident. Her memory was different from mine.

After months of recovery, my dad was able to work again, but never really the same physically. My brother eventually recovered and, at the age of seventeen, joined the Marine Corp. He became an officer, served in Vietnam, and then started his own company. Very smart guy.

My oldest sister, Jean, married at the age of sixteen, had six kids, but passed away from cancer in her early sixties. My sister, Linda, just four years older than me, became a distinguished teacher and worked at a school for troubled teens in Panama City. Also very smart.

My siblings were smart; my dad was smart (he actually came up with a design for a gas-less auto engine). So what happened to me? Somewhere between Linda and me the "smart gene" took an early lunch. I earned straight "A's" from first through sixth grade. But in grades seven through twelve, and then in college, achieving average was a success.

My mom worked as a waitress at almost every food facility in Panama City. As a result, I was left on my own from the age of five. In many ways it was challenging. Fun but challenging. My daughter tells me I had a Tom Sawyer childhood. But the reality was, I didn't know any different. That was the life I knew.

I have vivid memories of the woods just across the road from our house. The low-lying areas flooded during the rainy season and my best friend, Jerry Hood, and I would build rafts and go floating through the woods. It was common to see water moccasins swimming past us. Still to this day Jerry and I call each other by our last names; he's Hood to me, and I'm Green to him. Maybe it's because we're both named Jerry, so it's easier for others to keep us identified.

One of Hood's and my favorite foods was to deep-fry saltine crackers over an open fire. All that's needed is a match, fire wood, frying pan, lard, and saltine crackers … very healthy.

During a particularly dry summer, a fire burned much of the interior of the forest. As my mom left for work one morning she told me not to go into the woods. But what does a five year old do when older kids invite him to go with the "big boys"? He goes.

We walked through the woods, careful to avoid the smoldering piles of ash, and then I followed as they hopped onto a log to cross over an area scorched by the fire. At the end of the log they jumped across a pile of leaves, but I jumped onto the leaves. Underneath was smoldering, hot ash. I hit it and sank. The skin began burning from my bare feet and I found it impossible to move. I stood screaming, my hands grasping the log and my feet burning in the ash.

The older boys dragged me from the coals and one began carrying me out while the other ran home to get my sister. It was a long recovery. Since both feet were burned, I was confined to the couch for weeks, unless someone volunteered to carry me. Lesson learned: obey Mom.

Fortunately, burns heal over time. Unfortunately, lessons learned can fade. But my childhood always seemed to be filled with adventure.

Opening Scene 5

One of the chilling "could-have-beens" involved two neighborhood brothers I began hanging out with for a brief time. They encouraged me down a path that could have been disastrous. One evening they decided that we should steal six packs of soft drinks from a local convenience store. Another time they wanted to steal bags of empty soft drink bottles from a local church. In an ironic twist, someone stole the bottles from the location where we hid them.

I heard many years later that one of the brothers was on death row for murdering someone. Choosing friends can have significant consequences.

Another relationship that could have ended poorly for me was with a relative-in-law of my oldest sister, and another neighbor of ours. Ronny was several years older and took me hunting on a couple of occasions. But he, too, was later put on death row and hanged for killing several people in Kansas, around the same time as the events in Truman Capote's novel, *In Cold Blood*. Ronny and his accomplice were in the cell next door to the killers in Capote's book.

I could tell stories of carrying eggs in my pockets from our chicken coop and my sister pushing me against the wall, causing them to break; or breaking open watermelons in my dad's patch and eating just the heart of it; or often times running my toy car with a windup gears through my sisters long hair which could only be removed with scissors; or my sixth-grade teacher who allowed Hood and me to get away with way too much; or the pranks we pulled on our poor eighth-grade teacher during class, sending her out of the room crying; or walking five miles home from the theatre every Saturday when I was eight years old; or the time, as an eleven-year-old kid, I asked two girls to the same showing of the same movie—one in the balcony and one down below; or tying a neighborhood boy to a tree and setting it on fire (he was okay).

But I do recall one last incident that was perhaps a precursor to my theme-park career. My brother Wayne, my sister Linda, and I decided to build an amusement park. All the "rides" in our park were crude and, for the most part, dangerous. Our theme park included a seesaw, a flying jenny (which was just a post in the ground with a ten-foot 2x6 nailed across the top), a swing hanging from a tree limb, and a few other creative ideas that provided ample opportunity to kill yourself.

But the one ride that left an indelible imprint was the zip line. It was a metal cable suspended between two trees and an eight-inch metal pipe surrounding the cable for the rider to hold on to. There were no straps to secure the rider to the pipe. Just climb the tree, grab the metal pipe, and away you went ... really fast!

Take my word for this, there's absolutely no friction to slow the pipe, or the rider, when the metal pipe is on a metal cable. I'm reminded of the movie *Christmas Vacation*, where Chevy Chase sprayed a new friction-reducing lubricant on the bottom of his sled.

Our ride reached supersonic speed in seconds. It was a blur, and there was nothing to stop or slow the rider, except the tree hurtling toward you. It was bail off or ... actually the "or" was death. So it was bail or die! We should have given that a little more thought. Our slogan could have been: "Come, experience our theme park. You might not die." Youth and stupidity—sometimes a lethal combination.

So, how does a kid from the sticks in north Florida get to Hollywood?

My mom remarried when I entered my teens. After a couple of years, she and her new husband, Don, moved to Phoenix. Since I was under age, I was included in the relocation. I won't bore you with a side trip to Fort Worth for a year, or the move back to Panama City for a few months, but in the end I graduated from Phoenix Union High School and attended Phoenix College, where I majored in pre-law.

THE 1960s

Phoenix is only a six-hour drive to Hollywood, so in the summer of 1967 I had my first visit to the Golden State. Of course a person can't visit southern California without a trip to Disneyland, which was only twelve years old at the time, and the tour at Universal Studios, a mere three years old. While on the guided tour I saw Dan Blocker filming a movie on the back lot. (Google can help if you don't recognize that name.) But I was overwhelmed! A poor kid from the sticks saw a Hollywood movie star. I finally made it—my Deep South drawl intact.

A year later it was vacation time and you can probably guess where I wanted to go. My wife, Tracey, and I drove west for a return visit to Disneyland and Universal Studios. On this visit to Universal I was smitten. While there, I found out that applications for tour guides were being taken the following week. So, a week later, in the spring of 1968, I boarded a plane—my first plane ride I might add—and flew to Burbank, only a short drive to Universal and Hollywood.

Nervous? The closest I'd ever been to show biz was the local movie theatre in Panama City, except for the time Fabian came to our little town for a concert.

In the early days of the tour most of the offices were in trailers, such as mine when I became entertainment manager. (But we'll get to that in due time.)

I sat in the trailer/personnel office, waiting for my interview. A couple of people were in line ahead of me, so the wait was excruciating. Finally, I heard, "Jerry, come in and let's talk." My feeling was, "We don't need to talk, just give me the job." But I found the more we talked, the easier it became. They were there to help. I wish I could remember who interviewed me, because I owe my career to that person. They could have just as easily said, "You're a hick from the sticks. You aren't what we're looking for," and I would have retuned to Phoenix and my grocery clerk job.

Much to my surprise, I was hired on the spot. I don't think it had much to do with my effervescent personality, which I didn't possess. Perhaps it was a need for tour guides.

At that time, the tour was just four years old. It started when studio management began allowing Grayline buses to drive onto the lot and around the studio, then have lunch at the commissary. There wasn't much else to it at first. But oh brother, change was coming.

To truly appreciate how significant it was for anyone to drive through that main gate of the studio, you must remember that back then studios were strictly off limits to the public. Everything on the other side of that guard booth was a mystery except to the elite few who had access to the inside world of show biz. For the Smitty, the guard at the main gate, to raise that electric arm and motion you through, was a big deal. (Yes, it's true, Carl Laemmle allowed visitors to the studio when it first opened in 1915. For twenty-five cents guests could sit in bleachers around the sets and cheer for their favorite movie stars. But with the advent of sound that was no longer possible.)

I hadn't made it through the main gate yet because my interview was in the tour division at the top of the hill, separated from the lower lot. But I was close.

Anyway I was dazed when the interviewer said, "You're hired! Here's your training manual. You start Monday." Yikes! Monday? I had a job in Phoenix. Now what do I do? Yes, it was a dilemma, but the decision was easy. I wanted to be in show biz. I would find a way. So much for giving a two-week notice.

At this point I looked at the tour as a stepping stone on the way to becoming a great actor, the next Paul Newman or James Garner. I couldn't pass up the opportunity.

The Reader's Digest version of the story is that I hurried home, wrapped up things in Phoenix, and headed back to southern California.

They say (whoever "they" is) that most people fear public speaking more than anything in life. Some would rather die than have to speak from a public platform. I'm not sure the fear was that severe, but it was an anxious time as I showed up that first day for training.

What am I doing here? This is Hollywood. This is Universal Studios, in Universal City, California.

But here I was with eight or ten others on that early Monday morning. We first spent time getting to know each other, and I have to admit, I felt totally inadequate, inferior to everyone. I was training with Hollywood kids. They were training with a poor shlub from the South who used words like "ya'll." This was a lot different than collecting eggs from the chicken coop, or playing with my goat in Panama City, or washing cars (my first job in Phoenix), or stocking shelves at Bashas' Market in Phoenix.

Suck it up! I can do this. Memorize, memorize, memorize. The guided portion of the tour in those days was about an hour and a half in length. There was no video assist on the tram, and only one special effect. (The Flash Flood opened the year I started as a guide.) The tour guide was the tour! He/she either made it entertaining, or it was a bust.

I had long ago embraced the desire to be a student of show biz. I learned everything I could learn. I *wanted* to learn. Watching people like Steve Allen and Johnny Carson on late-night television helped hone my focus and sense of humor.

So I threw myself into it. When did Universal open? Who started it? How big was it? How many sound stages were there? Who owned it now? How many employees? Who was under contract? What TV shows were filming on the lot? What movies were filming? Where's the prop department? What's *in* the prop department? What does filming MOS mean? Who's in that tall black tower sitting adjacent to the front gate?

Those and a myriad of other questions would have to be answered in the next three or four days. But more than just learning information, more than just memorizing facts, I had to learn how to relay that information to a group of ninety people in an entertaining way. And I wanted to be good at it. I desired to be the best, but not in a selfish way at the exclusion of other guides.

From day one I treated the people on my tram, those who paid money to get inside the largest, busiest studio in the world, as honored guests. That feeling never changed in twenty-five years. They wanted to see show biz from the inside. And I got to be part of their experience. It was awesome!

Having an appreciation for the guests was the first of two keys I learned at an early show-biz-age. So what was the second? It's the one thing that helped in my tour guide presentation and later when I was developing and hosting live shows.

To be successful it was essential that I learn to view my tour-guide presentation, and later my shows, from the audience's perspective. I had to move from the tour-guide seat in front to the last row of the tram, or step off the stage and sit in the last row of the two-thousand or five-thousand seat theater. And it had to be done both mentally and physically; physically go sit in the audience and watch someone do what I did, or better yet, watch a recording of my performance.

Everything had to be evaluated from the audience perspective. I spent countless hours evaluating every aspect of performing. And timing ... timing was the key. A famous comedic actor was once asked if someone could be taught comedic timing. His answer—no. I'm not sure if that's true, but it was critical for me to understand it.

Going through the process physically and mentally was fundamental. How does the audience see the tour, or view me as the tour guide? Or how did they perceive shows like Adam-12 or Emergency or The Great Chase? What are they seeing and understanding? I was a student.

But there was a twist to the process. While the tour-guide narration began as a memorized narration, it evolved into more of an ad-lib experience. I learned to talk with the audience, not at them. I learned that playing off what was happening at the moment was much more fun for the audience, and me, than reciting a canned presentation. The facts relating to the studio could be worked into the conversation.

Hosting shows (or as we called it, directing), was the same. Shows were never scripted, even from day one. As a matter of fact, the narrative of shows I would later host was whatever I came up with on the fly. The last show we did, the Star Trek Show, was the exception. However, even though it began as a written narrative, it quickly evolved into mostly ad-lib. (A perfect example of being truly unscripted would come later when we opened the Airport '77 Show).

Tour guiding was the closest I came to doing a scripted presentation. But the written script served only as the foundation. To that I added new elements, kept those that worked, and wove them into the script. Those that didn't work were discarded. Believe me, when ad-libbing you quickly discover what doesn't work. And you usually find out in front of an audience of two thousand people. If the only sound you hear is crickets after telling a joke ... scratch that one and move on.

Johnny Carson was the master at getting a laugh after bombing with a joke. I remember one show when he told a joke that was followed by total silence. Not even crickets.

He reached up and thumped the boom-mic. "I just wanted to make sure I hadn't gone deaf."

The bottom line ... I wanted to do a great job. I wanted to be the best for the sake of those on my tram. I wanted them to leave excited about show business. I wanted them to love Universal, because I loved Universal. I was the studio's biggest fan.

So we studied, we memorized, we practiced, and we rode trams. Starting the second or third day we had our own tram so we could practice giving tours. We took turns practicing as the guide, while the other trainees listened and rehearsed quietly to themselves. I had no concept of ad-libbing at this point. This was all new to me so I stuck to the script.

Graduation day was a Friday. We finished the class and the instructor congratulated everyone. As we were leaving he said to me privately, "Go home and practice, practice, practice." In the hidden recesses of his heart he probably wasn't convinced I was ready, but he gave me the green light anyway. I was a tour guide at Universal Studios!

And so it began ... the first day, the first tour.

We were all nervous. It's one thing to give tours to fellow trainees, but another to hear the dispatcher say, "Jerry, your tram is on the right. Go get 'em." To be perfectly honest, I can't remember a thing that happened on the first tour.

I was terrified that I might forget something. But then someone said to me, "The guests don't know what they're supposed to hear, so they won't know if you leave something out." That's was true, and I appreciated the advice, but I wanted the guests to know everything. I didn't want to leave anything out.

Even though my first tour is a blurred memory, I came back with the same number of people I left with. I didn't lose anyone. So from that perspective, it was good.

The summer of 1968 was a time of refining my tour presentation. I enjoyed it immensely, although it could be challenging at times. When you finish your third tour of the day, and the dispatcher said, "Sorry, you gotta do a fourth," you had to really love the job to pull it off. By the middle of the fourth tour you didn't know if you were giving the guests new information or repeating something you said five minutes before. That fourth tour was the one that forced a mind-meld with the first three. Tour guiding was performing, and although it might seem low key, which in some respects it was, the adrenaline was always pumping. Four tours in one day meant six hours of a non-stop rush.

The fourth tour would usually send the guide into autopilot. We could give the tour while concentrating on something totally unrelated, like "Did I lock my keys in the car?" "Did I lock the front door when I left home this morning?" "Did I pay the rent?" "What are my plans for the evening?" I remember more than once looking at the folks on that fourth tour and asking, "Did I already say that?"

One of my fellow guides was taking a tour along Denver Street, one of several western towns on the backlot. He was focused on something unrelated to the tour, when he suddenly blurted into the microphone, "Oh ****!" That jolted him back to reality. He stopped, looked at the guests on his tram and said, "Folks, I'm so sorry. My job is in your hands."

Fortunately, the group was forgiving and Mike kept his job. As a matter of fact, he was promoted a few years later—because he was a good employee, not because he swore. As best I can remember, there was no company policy that required promoting swearers.

During these early months at the studio I reasoned that if I was going to be the next great movie star, I should learn to act. But where would be the best place to learn? Where should I study?

At that time there were a few good schools in Hollywood. "The Pasadena Playhouse is a good place to hone your craft," I was told. People like Charles Bronson, Raymond Burr, Gene Hackman, Dustin Hoffman, Eve Arden, and Carolyn Jones studied there.

Jeff Corey also had an excellent reputation for training actors. He was hard on his students, a lot of yelling, but produced results. His student list included James Dean, Anthony Perkins, Jane Fonda, and Jack Nicholson.

Estelle Harman was a third option. Estelle taught people like Rock Hudson, Bill Bixby, Tony Curtis, Sharon Gless, and Audie Murphy. Estelle had been head of new talent at Universal, and her approach came with much less yelling.

I chose option three and scheduled an interview at Estelle's school on La Brea Avenue in Hollywood. We talked for a while and then she handed me a script and asked me to read a couple of scenes with her.

If I said she was blown away by my reading, that would be a gross overstatement. I ran lines together, had little to no emotion, and honestly, sucked at it. I could tell she was underwhelmed. And frankly, even I knew how horrible it was.

However, being a lady of immeasurable patience, she took a different approach by asking me to read certain lines and told me what emotion she wanted. After many tries my readings were still not great. I was more relaxed, but probably still not very convincing. I'm not sure she saw potential, but maybe felt sorry for me, being a "dumb kid from the sticks."

As a result of Estelle's encouragement (and sympathy), she and I took the plunge and made the commitment. It was probably more of a plunge for her than me. But it was a great experience, not only for my nascent acting career but also my tour presentation and show-hosting that was still in the future.

During my early years, I worked feverishly to eliminate the drawl from my speech. I thought it would be best if I had what was referred to as a "Middle America" sound. No accent. I went back to Panama City a few years later to visit family, and my cousin commented, "Jerry, you sound like a Yankee." A Southerner referring to someone as a Yankee is rarely a compliment.

The early years of tour guiding were really special, and also unpredictable. The tour began atop the hill. Guests entered the lobby, followed the queue line down the ramp, and then boarded the tram. I always liked being tram-side to chat with the guests as they boarded. I enjoyed the interaction with them prior to the start of the tour.

The tour was divided into two parts—a guided tour that lasted about ninety minutes, followed by some unstructurd time when the guests were dropped off at the Entertainment Center. Here, the guests could spend as much or as little time as they wanted, seeing shows, eating, shopping, visiting the snow set, or the Ark Park Petting Zoo (in the early days).

The guided portion of tour began in the "turn around" (a large circular area by the lobby), and after a welcome from the guide there were the usual safety announcements: "Keep your hands and arms inside the tram. If anything falls out of the tram just pull the cord running along the top and we'll stop and pick it up, unless it's your mother-in-law. If that happens, pulling the cord is optional. We'll just keep driving. We try to be flexible." We also introduced the tram driver. "Everybody say hi to our driver, Chuck. We're really proud of him. This is his sixth day out of rehab and he's finally stopped having those fainting spells." Management frowned on those kind of comments, but we sometimes made them anyway. Most of the drivers went along with it.

The driver started the engine and slowly down the hill we went. Shortly after leaving the tour we made a turn and passed a full-sized cavalry fort used in several movies and TV shows. After that was the Rock Slide, further down was the Burning House, then the fire station, and past that the makeup department managed by John Chambers.

Aside from being an extremely talented, academy award winning makeup and prosthetic expert, John Chambers was a genuinely kind man, especially to the guides. Although his department wasn't a regular part of the tour, on occasion I would make a personal visit. John always took time from his busy schedule to talk and explain what he was doing and how he did it. He would say, "Hey Jerry. Yeah, we're really busy, but come on in. Let me show you this...." Even if I suggested coming back later, John would not have it. He always took time.

John was awarded the CIA's Intelligence Medal of Merit for his involvement in what came to be known as the Canadian Caper, when six American hostages escaped during the 1979 Iran hostage crisis. That true incident was the basis of the 2012 movie *Argo*. John Goodman played the part of John Chambers. John passed away in 2001, one month shy of his seventy-ninth birthday.

After the tour division passed its infancy we were assigned our own permanent sound stage, Stage 32. However, in the early days we were assigned a different stage each day to take the guests through. It just depended on which stage wasn't being used that day for filming. Some days we would visit one stage in the morning and a different one in the afternoon.

Every morning we received a shooting schedule from the lower lot, so we actually knew what was in production and where. The dispatcher would tell us, "Stage 17 this morning. *Ironside* just wrapped there yesterday." Or, "Stage 44. It's prepped for an *Adam-12* shoot tomorrow." These were actual working sets. The actors were there the day before or coming the following day.

It was common to see "Hot Set" signs on interior sets. We had to remind guests not to touch or move anything on the set, especially if the production crew was returning for a continuation shoot. If a guest moved a lamp from a coffee table in a scene shot yesterday and put it in a different location, and the crew came to following day to shoot again, when the two scenes were edited together the lamp would jump from one place to another. And that sort of thing happened. (Not because of the guests on my tour, of course.) The guests were always cooperative and excited to be on actual working sets.

However, there were times when stages with sets were occupied and we would be assigned a stage that was completely empty. Completely empty! Four bare walls and nothing else. And remember, it was typical for us to spend forty minutes or more inside the sound stage with the guests. When the tram dropped us off, a group just coming out of the stage would board that tram and continue their tour, or the tram would go back to the tour center for another group. So we were at the stage until another tram arrived to pick us up.

When stuck in an empty stage, the first thirty to forty minutes were easy, but it was amazing how much "creative" material we could come up with during the last, long fifteen minutes. The mind starts racing to come up with things to say. "Folks, let me tell you a secret about Paul Newman that nobody knows...." "Yeah, I remember the time when Steven Spielberg...." "Telly Savalas once came to me and asked...." A lot of Hollywood rumors may have been spawned by tour guides during that last fifteen minutes in the empty sound stage.

But the guests were enamored with the whole experience, even an empty sound stage. I think it had something to do with it all being authentic. It wasn't a "staged" scenario....

The sumer and fall of 1968 were wonderful seasons for developing new friendships—Barbara, John, Diane, Nancy, Susan, Andy, several Mikes, and Pam (that last name, attached to a different person, would come to play the most significant role in my life). Some became good friends. We occasionally shared a sound stage together, or hung out after work and partied together. (Although "partied together" seems to have a completely differently meaning today than it did back then.)

I remember one evening a group of us, maybe eight or ten, went to dinner at Bob's Big Boy in Toluca Lake, just five minutes from the studio. We sat talking in the back section of the restaurant. I can't remember the guy's name (which is a good thing), but suddenly he started yelling ...

at me ... in the restaurant! It wasn't a contained yell that only we could hear. It was yelling so everyone in the restaurant and neighborhood could hear. I had no idea what was going on since I was facing away from him talking with a female guide. But this idiot was yelling at me like I had just neutered his cat. At the conclusion of his tirade, he threw his napkin on the table, jumped up, and stormed out.

After a few minutes to get our heart rate back to normal, we paid the bill and slipped out. It was one of those exits where we knew everybody was thinking, "Glad those morons are leaving." But didn't they understand we were tour guides at Universal Studios? We were in show biz! Truth is, we hoped they didn't know we were connected to the studio. No one wanted to tarnish the studio's name, except the buffoon who left before us.

We went outside and the buffoon was leaning against his car as if everything was right with the world; as if the outburst never happened. I approached him, curious to hear why he went off on me, before I punched his ticket. His explanation was, "I always do that when I don't have money to pay for my food. It gives me a reason to leave without people focusing on the check."

I was pretty much committed to taking him out before hearing that, but such a stupid answer was like fuel to the fire. Rather than ask to borrow a few bucks, he....

I should stop here and explain. Back then, I had a short fuse with people like that. Fortunately for him, the calmness of others in the group prevailed and he left with all his teeth. Guess who I never dined with again, unless first seeing proof that he had money.

I remember going to see the movie *The Wild Bunch* with a guide friend named Bridget. Her father, Edmond O'Brien, was one of the stars in the movie, and every time her dad had a line of dialogue, be it funny or not, she would laugh so loud that everyone in the theater could hear. She was proud of her papa. It was a fun experience.

Another guide who had a famous daddy was Stacy, Jack Webb's daughter. A nephew of one of the Andrews Sisters was also part of our little cadre. Most everyone had a famous mom, dad, aunt, uncle, or third-cousin-twice-removed. Then there was me. I had a goat named Bill.

In looking back on my early days at the studio, there was one person in particular who stands out and became a lifelong friend. Our friendship spanned beyond the bounds of the studio as he continued to impact my life until his death in 2014. His name was Terry Winnick. Terry started at Universal in 1967, a year before me. But over the course of time we became like brothers. Terry made an indelible imprint on my life, like Jerry Hood, the friend from my childhood mentioned earlier.

Guides always got a special lift at the end of a tour if the audience applauded. It made us feel like we did a good job. Terry was different. He would tell his group, "If you enjoyed the tour, don't applaud, give me one of these...," then he would hold up his hand and make the "okay" sign with his fingers. It worked. He usually got the seal of approval.

The opening of Sheraton Universal Hotel was a milestone in the life of the studio. Disneyland had their hotel, and now we now had ours. We were moving up.

Several of the guides were asked to serve as hosts for the grand-opening party held in the tour center. Our job was to stand around and answer questions, give directions, and look welcoming. The studio was oozing celebrities. To borrow part of a line from the movie *Three Men and a Little Lady*, "You couldn't swing a dead cat without hitting a celebrity." Everywhere you turned was a star, and I was in the middle.

I recall tapping Monty Markham on the back and telling him how much I liked his television show. He looked at me like I was an idiot ... and why was I touching him? In his defense, he probably didn't mean it that way. But I didn't know any different; I was new at that kind of thing. (At that time, he was starring in a television show with Arthur O'Connell called *The Second Hundred Years*.)

On another occasion MCA (the parent company of Universal) hosted a big event at the Sheraton for music store owners and promoters from around the country for the company's two record labels, MCA and Decca. I was asked to serve as a host to the artists in the green room, a place for them to relax prior to going on stage. Our green room was just a couple of connected rooms upstairs in the hotel, and my job was to hang out in the outer room and smile. We provided snack foods, water, and soft drinks.

First up was Bill Cosby. He entered and walked into the second room without an acknowledgement, then stretched out on the bed to watch the Lakers game. After a few minutes I stuck my head in and asked what the score was. He answered, but seemed annoyed with my intrusion. I guess he needed his space. Okay, I get it.

The second performer was Neil Diamond. He didn't come to the green room before his performance, but since there was no one in the room, I snuck downstairs to catch the last few minutes of his show. It was great.

Just as he finished and stepped off stage I hurried back to the elevator so I could get upstairs just in case he decided to come up. As I got in the elevator, guess who stepped in also? Neil Diamond. He was most gracious and we chatted for a while on the ride up the elevator. He confessed that his voice was a little out of shape, but it didn't sound like it to me. (My wife and I saw him in concert many years later. He still had it!)

Most mornings I would get to the studio early before the crowds arrived and just stroll around. Mornings in the park were special, always quiet and peaceful, and the view overlooking the San Fernando Valley was beautiful. You could see for miles.

The morning following my elevator encounter with Neil Diamond, I strolled the park (we referred to the Entertainment Center where the shows were located as "the park"). As I did so, guess who I ran into? My good friend Neil Diamond. (At least that's how I remembered the relationship.)

Neil was alone, casually strolling around like me, enjoying the scenery and the serenity. Again he was most gracious. By that time a few guests began arriving in the park, and the interesting thing was, people from Duluth, Des Moines, Decatur, and other cities beginning with a "D" strolled by without realizing they were passing one of the most famous recording artists in the world. I mean, really—"Holly Holy," "Sweet Caroline," "Cherry Cherry." Some of the best!

It wasn't uncommon to see Robert Wagner and Natalie Wood in the park. They were big fans ... of mine, not the park. You may be thinking that my perception of celebrity encounters was a little jaded, but that's how I remember it. Neil and Robert might have a different recollection, or more likely, no recollection at all. Years later, at Universal Florida, I would work with Robert Wagner (or RJ as his friends call him) on a promotional film for the studio.

The first years of the tour were very special. It was a new venture—a new *ad*venture. It had never been done. We were making it up as we went. Mistakes? You bet! Lots of them. But MCA/Universal management was experimenting, and for the most part, they allowed us to experiment, too.

The tour narration learned during training was the foundation for my narrative, but only a foundation. As mentioned earlier, my tour, as with most guides, evolved into mostly ad-lib, interaction with the guests, finding what worked—and just as important, what didn't. And believe me, there was plenty that didn't. I learned to watch what was happening and play off that.

I recall once when taking a group through the sound stage, I was giving them my best material, lines that were sure winners, proven laugh getters. But there was nothing from their side. Stone-faced! I had chatted with them earlier during the boarding process, and when I commented on something along the tram route, they looked in the direction I was referring to. So even though they were not from the US, I knew they spoke English. But there was silence on jokes I had used countless times before. And I tried them all. Finally, I paused, stared them in the eye, and said, "This is the first time I've ever seen dead people sit up." Guess what? They laughed. I guess they liked dead jokes.

Interesting that after all these years, I still remember that particular "dead group."

And, by the way, they did have a good time. They were very friendly and appreciative after the tour. Perhaps their lack of response had something to do with cultural differences in humor. It taught me to adjust my material to the audience. Sarcasm can be funny, but it usually helps to first build a rapport. The "dead people sitting up" line may not have been funny if I had said it before building the bridge.

That kind of ad-libbing would become taboo as the tour grew. As we got bigger, there was a need for more guides. More guides required more management. The result of more management was less freedom to ad-lib. The close personal relationship we enjoyed was lost as the number of employees grew. That's not a complaint. It's a natural result of growth. But by the time those changes came I had moved on to other areas of the studio.

In the early years we guides were few in number, so management knew and trusted us. Rather than "Guide 47, your tram is on the right," it was, "Jerry your tram is on the right. And by the way, I heard about your 'dead people sitting up' line. Funny!" Okay, so maybe I'm exaggerating about Guide 47, but you get the point.

Our small cadre of guides was committed to assuring that the guests always had a good time. And by the way, I never called our visitors "tourists." To us they were always guests. And later when I became a manager, I insisted on the same respect from those under my supervision. I don't mean to sound exclusively altruistic. The Uni guides, on whole, genuinely cared.

In the early years of the tour it was common to see actors, actresses, and tech people walking around the studio. When I first started as a guide, Paul Newman was on the lot after filming *The Secret War of Harry Frigg*. He usually parked his little red VW in the hub, a large open area where trams stopped and guests disembarked for a tour through Stage 32. The hub was encircled by Edith Head's office on one side; Raymond Burr's dressing room adjacent to that; one of the prop department buildings; Stages 28, 32, and 34; and roads leading from the main gate and other areas of the studio.

Edith Head was another extremely accommodating person to tour guides. She was friendly, helpful, and usually took time to wave to the guests as she hurried from one project to another. She always seemed to be a frail-looking, but peppy little lady who was forever in a hurry.

I remember sitting on the tram in the hub and seeing a character actor passing a short distance away. I said into the microphone, "Ladies and gentlemen, there's actor Brian David." He casually walked over and I leaned down from the tour-guide seat, which was elevated at the front of the tram. He whispered, "It's David Brian." Ooops! Sorry, Mr. Brian. He wasn't offended by me getting his name wrong. He corrected my error in a very kind way that only I could hear. At least I got the right names, just in the wrong order.

Raymond Burr was also a friend to the tour, always ready to wave and smile. But we did have others who were not user friendly. They were on the "don't point out" list.

Yes, there was a such a list. Some spent way too much time reading their own press clippings. Shirley McLaine comes to mind. She did entertain the guests one day by mooning everyone as the tram passed by. James Drury was also a definite no-no. He threatened to walk off the set if another guide pointed him out. Robert Blake, same thing.

I was told by an interior decorator friend of mine that at the height of the TV show *Baretta*, the studio spent a large sum of money decorating Blake's dressing room; special carpet, décor from Europe, etc. Blake walked into the room for the first time, looked around, spat on the floor, then walked out.

For the sake of convenience, the transportation department parked trailers (mobile dressing rooms) in the hub. After guests got off the tram, but before taking them through the sound stage, we spent a few minutes orienting them to the location and the significance of the hub.

Part of my spiel included talking about the dressing rooms. "You have to understand," I would tell my group, "there's a pecking order when it comes to being assigned a dressing room. Stars like John Wayne, James Garner, Loretta Lynn, Charlton Heston, get the plush dressing rooms like the one Raymond Burr has" (point to his dressing room behind them). "Next in the chain are character actors, Tom Ewell, E.G. Marshall, and others like that. They, too, get a dressing room, perhaps not quite as nice. Then there are the day players, people who have a few lines and work for just a day or two. They get a trailer, but it's still their own private space. Next come people who do 'walk ons'; no lines, they just walk through a scene. They share a room with several other actors of the same stature. Then come the tour guides. We dress behind cars, under trees, behind buildings, anywhere we can find a spot."

After touring the sound stage the group reboarded the tram and drove through the prop department. Universal's prop department housed over 5,000,000 props and covered more than an acre of land. Fortunately, the road through the warehouse was large enough to accommodate trams. There were countless set decorations and show pieces on both sides of the tram, so everyone had a good view. Warehouses were filled with props from Universal movies and TV shows, many of them recognizable. A photographer's dream. On rare occasion we were allowed to walk through the department since it was next to the hub, near Stage 32.

Coming out of the prop department the tour route turned and headed to the exterior sets on the backlot, passing what was referred to as Wall Street. This street was merely rows and rows of walls that could be assembled in any configuration to create interior rooms or exterior walls.

Just ahead, Anytown, USA. Its official name was Colonial Street, one of my favorite streets. We called it Anytown because it could be made to represent any town in America. It had many, many names over the years, depending on what was being filmed. Perhaps the most famous residents at the time were the Cleavers. It was home to Wally and the Beaver from *Leave It to Beaver*. Many years after that show ended, Jerry Mathers, the Beaver, became one of our Celebrity of the Day persons.

Thirteen-thirteen Mockingbird Lane. Sound familiar? I remember the address after all these years. But shortly after the Beaver and Wally moved out, the Munsters moved in. Fred Gwynne, Yvonne De Carlo, and Al Lewis set up residence just a few doors down from where the Cleavers had lived. Al Lewis, Grandpa Munster, eventually became a Celebrity of the Day as well.

The Cleavers would soon move out, and the Munsters had not yet arrived, when James Garner and Doris Day moved into the little community. Actually, they were right next door to the Cleavers, in one of my wife's favorite movies, *The Thrill of It All*. The house was where James Garner drove his car through the garage and into their new backyard swimming pool. The exterior scene was shot at that house, but the backyard scene was filmed in a sound stage. They built a full-size pool inside the stage. Garner drove through the garage and into the pool that was surrounded with boxes of laundry detergent. Sounds weird, but catch the movie and you'll understand.

Perhaps the most famous star-turned-politician to film on Colonial Street was Ronald Reagan in *Bedtime for Bonzo*. The movie was directed by Fred de Cordova, who later became executive producer for *The Tonight Show Starring Johnny Carson*. As a matter of fact, Carson used to make comments about de Cordova's chimp experience. (Bonzo, of course, was a monkey.)

The truth is, that little street, just over a quarter mile long, saw more actors, camera crews, food trucks, and honey wagons (portable restrooms) than could be counted. It *was* Anytown, USA.

One of the early films shot there and released in 1927 was called *Uncle Tom's Cabin*. The same house, the first one on the left as you entered the street, was also used in 1960 for *Inherit the Wind*, with Spencer Tracey, Fredric March, Gene Kelly, and Harry Morgan.

In 1981 many of the houses on the street were moved elsewhere on the back lot, closer to the Psycho House. The new location was home for *Desperate Housewives*.

Leaving Anytown, USA, the tour headed toward New York Street, the brownstone area, then turned and crossed the Collapsing Bridge, a special effect designed by Terry Winnick.

Prop Plaza was a mid-way stop on the guided tour. It was just up from the Collapsing Bridge, above the "greens area" where trees were kept in oversized boxes so they could be transported anywhere on the studio property. Did you ever wonder how a studio was able to shoot a summer scene that required a green lawn and trees, but was filmed in fall or winter when everything was brown? Simple, just spray paint the lawn. Instant green lawn and trees. I also recall hearing of times when the greens department had to glue or staple leaves onto trees because the leaves had fallen off.

By the time we reached Prop Plaza, it was an hour into the guided tour—a good time for a break. At Prop Plaza guests could get food, visit restrooms, and take pictures of family members lifting oversized foam rubber boulders, standing next to the war wagon from John Wayne's movie of the same name, or sitting in a rocking stagecoach with a moving background behind it.

Guests were required to exit the tram at Prop Plaza. "Folks, you will need to exit the tram. You can grab food and visit the restrooms, and when you're ready to reboard the tram, make your way to the boarding area. There you'll get a different guide and continue the second half of your tour. There are lots of photo opportunities here so take all the pictures you want, just don't take the ones hanging on the walls." Corny, but it worked.

Guests disembarked and the tram drove to the loading elevation, which was on the opposite side and slightly down from the drop-off. There we would pick up a new group.

I think one of the reasons I strove to be the best guide I could be was so no one on my tour would think the guide they got the second half of the tour was better. Maybe a little ego is hidden in there somewhere. But it pushed me to strive to be the best.

Remember, all the while we were giving tours, the studio was busy filming movies and television shows in locations across the lot. Although there were times when there was no filming, it wasn't uncommon for security personnel to flag our tram to wait for a scene that was shooting near our route, maybe on New York Street, Courthouse Square, Spartacus Square, or any of a hundred different locations. We would whisper in the microphone, "Folks, please be very quiet. They're filming *Kojak* just ahead. Keep a look out, you might see Telly

Savalas." Everyone was always very cooperative. I never had anyone on my tour or heard of any others having an issue with an uncooperative guest. If the tram wasn't moving, guests would stand and strain to get a view. And if Savalas was available, he would always wave and smile. He was on the "it's okay to point out" list.

As the summer rush wound down I was promoted to show announcer in the Entertainment Center. My job was to introduce the Wild West Stunt Show, Animal Actors Show, a marionette show, and a pantomime show. Yes, there was a pantomime show with Antonine Hodek. And no, there was never a long wait to get into that show. But, those who saw it liked it. I guess it could be remembered as "cute." There were two other shows (or demonstrations) in the Entertainment Center, but neither required an announcer.

The narration for Wild West Stunt Show began with: "Good afternoon, ladies and gentlemen and welcome to the Wild West Stunt Show. Today we are pleased to have with us actor/stuntmen currently working in the motion picture and television industry. I'd like to introduce to you one of those gentleman now. He just completed work on (name of movie or TV show). Would you please welcome actor/stuntman Lance Rimmer." The audience applauded as Lance burst through the saloon doors and jogged across the stage. I handed off the microphone and the show was under way. It was an exciting and entertaining show.

The stunt show was initially located in the back of the park. There were no seats in the theater, only rails for the audience to lean against. Although the viewing area was tiered, it presented a challenge for short people, unless they were in the front. Seats would eventually be added and the theater would become home to Stage 70, later renamed the Screen Test show, and moved to a new location.

The original stunt show, prior to Lance joining the team, was entertaining but not great. The set consisted of three attached buildings, two stories each—a general store, a saloon, and a hotel—looking left to right from the audience.

When the show moved to the new location Lance's creative juices kicked in and it became a hall of famer. At one point, management decided the show needed a quicksand pit, which Lance always considered unnecessary. But he was a faithful employee and incorporated the pit into the show, and even figured a way to get a laugh with it.

The original stunt show, however, featured Arnold Roberts (he always reminded me of Lee Van Cleef) as the "mic man" and the show was considerably different from the version that would later come with Lance, Gray Johnson, and Norman Dell.

After the introduction, Roberts would burst through the saloon doors, draw his revolver, and fire a shot straight at the audience twenty-five feet away.

Probably not the best way to start a show, for a couple of reasons. One, beginning with a "bang" gave away one of the show's building blocks. It's good to save bangs, loud noises, and surprises for later. Every element of the show—a gun shot, a bull whip crack, a breaking bottle, a thrown punch—should build to a climax; in the case of the stunt show, all elements built up to the finale ... a high fall.

But the second reason not to fire a shot at the audience was—blanks! The blank shells used in the guns had a small wadding of paper that, when fired, was propelled from the barrel of the pistol with significant force. I witnessed, on more than one occasion, the paper wad hit an audience member standing in the first or second row. A few years later a stuntman named Steve Gillum was struck in the eye from a greater distance and suffered permanent damage.

How did the show transition from a small, mildly entertaining show to the most popular show ever on the tour? The transition began when Arnold Roberts and his team went to Texas for a promotion of some kind.

Lance was doing a stunt "demonstration" with a couple of guys at 20th Century. (It was a walking tour and nothing on the scale of Universal.) Our operation's manager, Cliff Walker, asked Lance to bring some guys and fill in while Roberts' team was away. Lance showed up and after a couple of days, being the consummate *stager* that he was, decided to make some "minor" changes. So he added a few comedic elements.

I don't think I ever told Lance, but I remember thinking, "Who does this guy think he is? Coming here to fill in and changing our show."

At this time, I was relatively new and inexperienced in staging, timing, and show development, but it didn't take an entertainment genius to see that the few minor changes Lance made were a significant improvement.

Lance was the best I ever saw at staging shows. He had an innate gift to look at a set/stage and come up with a complete show in a relatively short time. Or he could watch an existing show and immediately give ideas that would work better. I learned a lot from him.

Lance's minor changes ended up being a total rework of the show. Big problem! Jay Stein, president of MCA Recreation Services, heard of it. MCA Recreation Services was the tour division of the parent MCA/Universal.

Later that day Lance got a call: "John Lake's office, now!" (John was the general manager.) Lance walked in and there sat Jay Stein, John Lake, Ron Harmon (entertainment supervisor), and someone else, perhaps Terry Winnick.

Jay cut to the chase, "Who the **** do you think you are changing my ******* stunt show?!" (Those who worked for Jay were convinced that he wrote the "Sailor's Guide to Colorful Communicating.")

Lance replied, "The audience likes it."

Jay turned to Ron Harmon.

Ron commented, "I don't like a comedy stunt show."

"But it isn't about what you like," Lance told him. "It's what the audience likes. And it isn't a comedy stunt show. It's a stunt show with humor."

Lance was right, and there *is* a difference.

However, the bottom line was that Lance, without permission, changed a show that was already successful. So, what to do? Based on audience response, Lance was right.

Jay decided to bring in an independent company to conduct a survey; two weeks of doing the old stunt show, two weeks of doing the new, humorous stunt show. (Jay was a firm believer in doing surveys, lots of surveys.) If the humorous show proved more popular than the old show, Lance could keep the new version, and his job. The end result—the show with humor was a smash hit and Lance was the golden child.

He was in charge of the stunt show for many years and always required the stuntmen do it the *right* way. And yes, the *right* way was *his* way. Don't improvise. Improvising in one area affected the timing of the show as a whole.

I remember, more than once, Lance reprimanding the comic for dragging out a laugh. Even if the audience was laughing, there was a time to cut it off; otherwise, it affected the next element of the show.

My show announcing days were terrific. I loved doing it. However, with four shows to introduce multiple times a day, I often found myself running from one show to the next—close the stunt show and hustle across the park to the animal show. "Good afternoon, ladies and gentlemen," pant, pant, deep breath, "welcome to the Animal Actors Show...." Believe me, it was exhausting at times. (I know "exhausting" is a relative term. When I was fifteen years old I worked as a roofer in the hot, humid Florida weather. Both roofing and show announcing were exhausting, just in a different way. And one was a lot more fun than the other.)

One of the many side benefits of announcing was that between shows, when time allowed, I hung out with the performers and goofed around. I learned to play the guitar from a fellow show announcer, and became fairly proficient with a bullwhip. I could flick the button on a coat, or take a cigarette out of someone's mouth—when I could find a person brave enough to let me try. Not only did he teach me how to use the whip, but Norman Dell was the one who held the cigarette in his mouth. (Norm passed away several years ago.)

An excellent team of stuntmen was assembled through the years including Jim Winburn, Tom Morga, John Casino, Chip Campbell, Wayne Bauer, Ray Woodfork, Carl Ciarfallio, Doc Duhame, Bill Oliver, Bob Rochelle, and Ray Gabriel. The problem with naming names is that someone is always forgotten, and I know I'm forgetting lots of quality performers. Sorry, guys.

It was always a special treat for the guests to see a "movie star" when visiting the studio. However, because much of the filming on the lower lot was inside sound stages, there was never a guarantee of seeing a celebrity. So we hired actors as "Celebrity of the Day" in the Entertainment Center. A few minutes prior to the stunt show I would introduce our guest star. The celeb would come out and spend five minutes talking with the audience. The audience loved it.

Two actors who worked most frequently as guest celebrities were Bob Hastings from *McHale's Navy* and Terry Wilson from *Wagon Train*. On occasion others would visit—Mike Farrell from *Days of Our Lives* (later to star as B.J. Hunnicutt in *M*A*S*H*); Huntz Hall, one of the original Dead End Kids, also known as The Bowery Boys; Ricardo Montalbán, star of *Adventurers in Paradise* (later to star as Mr. Roarke in *Fantasy Island*; and Scatman Crothers, an actor, singer, and dancer. Scatman was the livery stable owner in John Wayne's last movie, *The Shootist*, and also had a prominent role in *The Shining*.

One of the audience favorites was Bob Denver, Gilligan from *Gilligan's Island*. Bob was great with the audience, and usually wanted to take part in the show. And when he did, it was a crowd pleaser.

The Celebrity of the Day program ended when the stunt show moved to another location. It was re-instated years later at the Screen Test Theater.

The Animal Actors Show functioned differently from other shows in that it was a contracted show owned by Ray Berwick. Performers in other shows, except the marionette show, were employees of the studio. Universal provided the stage, but Ray owned the animals, and the animal trainers worked for him. Ray, and those who worked for him, were all very active in the industry, doing TV shows and movies.

One day, when introducing the animal show, I grabbed the microphone and walked on stage."Good afternoon, ladies and gentlemen. Welcome to Animal Actors Show. We have with us today several famous and talented animal stars from motion pictures and television. I would like to introduce to you one of Hollywood's most renowned animal trainers, the man responsible for training the birds used in Alfred Hitchcock's movie *The Birds*. Please welcome...." Blank! My mind went completely blank. I had nothing. I could not remember Ray's name. What to do? Without saying his name I said, "Let's welcome him now!", then turned and gestured behind me as Ray made his entrance with a huge grin on his face. He took the microphone and said, "Ray Berwick." I turned back to the audience, shrugged my shoulders, and smiled. Ray never let me forget that.

This was one of the few times I turned back to the audience after I started the show. When introducing someone,

I would say their name, then turn and face them, gesturing with my hand in their direction. This forced the audience's attention to the person coming on stage, rather than me.

Ray wasn't just a run-of-the-mill trainer, he was the biggest name in the industry when it came to movie and TV animals. He trained Benji, Fred the Cockatoo from the TV series *Baretta*, and a plethora of other Hollywood animal celebs. He was no light weight. He, along with his assistants Gary Gero and Brian Renfro, were considered the best. I just couldn't remember his name for that particular show on that particular day.

I recall walking through the park early one morning before the guests arrived, and saw Ray hurrying in my direction. He looked very somber, which was not like him. His eyes were red so we passed with just a nod. Later that day I found out that during the night a fox had gotten into one of the cages and killed his prize crow used in *The Birds*. That bird was very special to Ray, and one we used every day in the show. He was devastated.

The backlot was a refuge to wildlife—deer, fox, rabbits, snakes, and other creatures. From time-to-time they made their way up the hill and wandered into the Entertainment Center. One day, as Terry Winnick drove up the hill to the tour center, a deer jumped across the road right in front of him. He smashed into it, completely destroying the front of his car. The deer didn't fair all that well either.

Now you may wonder, why would anyone be interested in, or why would a studio think anyone would be interested in, a marionette show as one of its anchor productions? At first that was my thought also, but it was a very good show. It had its own theater, the Woody Woodpecker Theater (named as such because of its exhibit devoted to Walter Lantz's Woody Woodpecker), which it later shared with Antoine Hodek's short-lived pantomime show. The theater seated about a hundred and twenty people. It was a contracted show, owned by Tony Urbano, a master in the world of marionettes/puppets.

Rather than operate the marionettes from behind a curtain, Tony and another puppeteer would stand on stage beside the marionette and perform. It seemed odd the first time I saw it, but as I watched, the performers took on the personality of the marionette, or maybe it was vice-versa, and the two became one. You forgot the marionette wasn't doing it all itself. The facial expressions of the puppeteers seemed to translate to the marionettes.

Tony relayed the story that early in his career he turned down an invitation from a relative unknown at the time, Jim Henson. Tony was invited to go to Manhattan and work on a new show Henson was putting together. The show? *Sesame Street*.

The Marionette Show was one that required an announcer. One day I got to the theater a few minutes before show time. One of the two puppeteers had not yet arrived and we knew he wasn't going to make it in time for the show. What to do? The other performer and I agreed—the show must go on. "Jerry, put on the tuxedo (the marionette performers always wore a tux) and grab the marionette. You're going on!" I was about to earn my wings without first taking the lessons.

However, I had seen the show so many times I knew it by heart. That's not to say Jim Henson came knocking afterwards, but we got through it and the audience was none-the-wiser. When the show was over I even got a compliment from the other performer, and two of the marionettes. (I'm not sure Tony ever knew about my stealth performance.)

Tony gave me advice about audiences and applause. He felt that it was wise to step in and start talking shortly after the applause reached its peak, in effect cutting the applause short. The logic was that it left the audience feeling as if they still owed the performers more.

Three dramatic changes took place in my life at this point. First, in the midst of pursuing my career—announcing shows, meeting celebrities, and forgetting names—I became a father, after two years of marriage to Tracey. Kimberly Karis (she now spells it Kimi—apparently that's cooler) was born at Kaiser Hospital in Hollywood, California, in the wee hours of the morning. Why is it always in the wee hours of the morning?

Second, Tracey and I split up. But not because of Kimi. She was the delight of my life. But I was too focused on the biz, and less on what was really important. However, being a single guy meant I needed a place to live because I couldn't afford an apartment by myself. So I got a place with four other guides on Laurel Canyon Boulevard, just off the 101 Freeway in Studio City.

And third, just as my career at Universal was taking root, I received an invitation to join another group. After a year and a half at the studio, Uncle Sam called. I was drafted. So off I went to Fort Lewis, Washington, just outside Seattle, for eight weeks of basic training.

It rains in Seattle, a lot! Basic training was challenging, but good discipline. Shaved head, three meals a day, KP duty, drills, and exercise—lots of exercise. All of that while it poured rain. I remember being awoken one night while on bivouac because my tent had blown off and rain was pounding on my head. I remember my drill sergeant's name—Guzman. I remember qualifying as expert with M14 and M16 rifles. I remember, after six weeks of nothing but mess-hall food, we were allowed a trip to the base PX (a small grocery story that served milk shakes). I remember thinking as I slurped down my second shake that I had died and gone to heaven. I remember graduating from basic training weighing more that I ever had before: 182 pounds.

I completed basic training and was ready for my first assignment. The Army reasoned that since I was a show host at Universal Studios, I should go to "hosting school" in the Army. Frankly, I didn't know the Army had a great need for that sort of thing, but who was I to argue. They were being good to me so far. I graduated from Basic as one of three promoted to private with one stripe.

I was ordered to Fort Huachuca, Arizona, an hour south of Tucson. I was going to learn how to host an event, the Army way. Funny thing, upon arriving at Fort Huachuca I was told the Army had moved the "hosting school" several years earlier to somewhere on the East Coast.

Someone forgot to tell the Army that the Army moved its school.

What were they going to do with Private Green? I anticipated getting orders not to unpack because I was being reassigned to the East Coast. Not so fast, soldier. The person assigned to hand out jobs told me they had a job at Fort Huachuca that was similar to show hosting. Oh, really? I was going to be a reporter for the local base newspaper.

How could anyone argue with that kind of logic? I could see the connection.... But that's the closest job they had to hosting. It was that kind of reasoning that helped us *not* win the Vietnam War. (Just kidding.)

But before you jump to conclusions and think, "How boring!" just know that I covered breaking news like baking cookies at the base bakery. I could, but won't, tell the story of sweat dripping from the end of the cook's nose into the batter as the lieutenant gave the photographer and me a tour through the kitchen. (Guess what I no longer ate while on base. Everything! I figured if it was in the cookies, it was probably in everything else. Fortunately, the small town of Sierra Vista was next to the front gate and had a coffee shop.)

I also covered the monthly parade. Although it was a routine assignment every month, for a guy like me who loves his country, watching the troops march across the parade field past the flag with music blaring in the background produced goose bumps every time.

When I was granted a leave of absence during my two-year military stint, I usually returned to the southern California and visited the studio. Terry Winnick and his mom, dad, and brother, Jeff, always put me up for a few days so I didn't have to cover hotel expenses. It was at this point our friendship, like Jerry Hood's and mine when we were kids, began to develop into more of a "brothership."

To sum up Army life: I wasn't thrilled to be drafted, but oh so glad for the experience of serving. It was a milestone in my life.

As my two years of military life drew to a close I wrote Cliff Walker, operations manager at Universal, and told him I was getting out and wanted to come back to the studio.

I was honorably discharged with the rank of specialist five (equivalent to sergeant) in September 1971, two months shy of my full-two-year requirement. The military sometimes gave early discharges back then. I headed to Agua Dulce, California. Try finding that without a GPS.

THE 1970s

October 1971. The busy season was winding down at the studio, so I spent only a short time as a tour guide. I had to relearn the guide presentation because things had changed. Additions had been made.

Before I left for the Army the studio tour was fairly straightforward. A ninety-minute presentation and not much else. No fancy stuff aside from the Flash Flood and Torpedo Attack. But now there were "things," special effects to enhance the guest experience. That was good. I could adapt.

Another important change had taken place during my absence. Terry Winnick had completed his architectural degree at USC and moved from the entertainment side of the tour to full-time management. He was the go-to guy for building stuff. Think "special effects" during the first fifteen years of the tour—then put Terry's face with it. He was the man. He spent countless nights at the studio slaving over a hot slide rule and never made it home. If confirmation is needed just ask Barri, one of our fellow tour guides, and his wife for many years.

Terry also indirectly oversaw the entertainment department. He reported to John Lake, the general manager, and to Jay Stein.

In the midst of everything I still had the dream of being the next Paul Newman. So I began taking theater arts' classes again, this time at Valley College, and later at Cal State University, Northridge.

Looking back on the addition of special effects to the tour route, the early attempts might seem simple when compared to today's super high-tech robotics. But remember, just as silent movies in their day were cutting-edge technology, so was our Torpedo Attack and Burning House in their day. The Rock Slide, Collapsing Bridge, and Parting of the Red Sea added a slightly more sophisticated element to the tour. We were growing, "going where no man had gone before." (That quote would later become a reality at the Screen Test Theater.)

The simplicity of our first special effect was not due to a lack of knowledge on Terry's part. He would later design sophisticated cutting-edge rides and special effects. It was the learning curve that the tour as a whole was going through. It was also a matter of budgets. For the most part we were still an unproven commodity in the minds of Jules Stein (no relation to Jay), Lew Wasserman, and Sid Sheinberg.

I met Jules Stein a few times before his death in 1981. And although we didn't hang out together, he always treated us with respect. I remember Mrs. Stein as a lady who dressed like the queen of England. Her husband was fastidious but didn't dress like the king.

In defense of those charged with designing special effects, some things look good on paper but fail to have the desired result when completed. The most striking example of "not living up to the hype" was Jaws. I know, the Jaws ride in Orlando had its fan base, but for those present during the corporate sponsorship meetings prior to Universal Florida opening, they understand what I mean by "not living up to the hype," as I'll explain shortly.

A favorite special effect of mine was the Rock Slide. It was the kind of effect you had to love. Why? It was fun to watch, and it happened just five minutes into the guided tour. The hillside was covered with a man-made material resembling dirt. At the top of that hill was a container about 50–60 feet wide, and resembling a long dumpster, although we were not supposed to refer to it as a dumpster. Inside were large foam-rubber "boulders."

As the tram approached the area, guests would hear rumbling. The container at the top of the hill would rise from a pit sending the rocks careening down the hillside and coming to rest in a cleverly concealed trough next to the tram.

To no one's surprise, foam rubber has weight. So as the boulders made their journey down the seventy-five to one-hundred-foot hill, the rocks gained momentum ... and speed. Need I say, not all the rocks went into the container at the bottom. It was common to see rocks bounce over the trough and into or even through the tram. And yes, from time to time a guest would get smacked in the head by a boulder traveling at an impressive speed. We found that people sitting close together in a confined row on the tram can still move very quickly when the need arises, bobbing and weaving to avoid becoming part of the effect.

Now add rainy days to that scenario. The rocks sat in the trough at the top of the hill soaking up rain. After all, they were foam rubber. As the rocks rolled down the hill, a little rooster tail of water would flip up behind and leave marks each time it made contact with the ground. Although the rocks took longer to get up to speed, by the time they reached the bottom they were lethal.

If a rock skipped over the trough and made contact with a guest, it left a lasting souvenir. It was fun to watch. Eventually, we put an employee in that area to pick up boulders that missed the trough and put them back, as well as occasionally a guest.

The Torpedo Attack took place in Park Lake where *McHale's Navy* was filmed. The TV show starred Ernest Borgnine, Joe Flynn, and a genius of comedy, Tim Conway, and the aforementioned Bob Hastings. This effect involved an object resembling a torpedo cruising atop the surface of the water. As the "torpedo" approached the tram, an air cannon exploded, shooting water high into the sky. "Explode" is a strong word for what actually happened, but I'm trying to make it sound exciting.

Another special effect that deserves note is the Parting of the Red Sea. After experiencing the Torpedo Attack, the tram drove to the edge of the water at the far end of Park Lake and stopped. The "sea parted" and the tram drove through as water churned on both sides.

Guides were never supposed to refer to the "parting" of the Red Sea as such, but it was more like it *flushed*. I understand management's reasoning in forbidding the use of the word flushing, as the Flushing of the Red Sea didn't have the same magical appeal.

The effect was simple in its execution—two walls approximately fifteen feet apart, and slightly shorter than the water level, created a path for the tram to drive through. With the walls hidden just beneath the surface, they were camouflaged from the guests. A large drain in the bottom of the narrow path opened, the water quickly drained, and the tram drove through. The water level in the lake was a few inches higher than the 'invisible' walls, so water constantly cascaded over the edges. In theory it looked like the water was being held up, like in the movie *The Ten Commandants*, with Charlton Heston.

Sounds innocent, right? It was ... usually. But on occasion a glitch happened and the "sea" began refilling before the tram got out. And the effect refilled quickly. We only lost a few guests....

Seriously, the worst that happened was people got wet. The trams could move quickly when necessary. But we found the guests could move even quicker climbing onto their seats. When those glitches happened, the tour guide's reminder to "remain seated at all times when the tram was in motion" was ignored.

Park Lake was the site for filming the 1954 black-and-white 3D monster horror film, *The Creature from the Black*

Lagoon. Nothing says realism like a 3-D movie in black and white. The first Tarzan movies with Elmo Lincoln were also shot in that location.

After touring the exterior sets, passing the Flash Flood, Six Points Texas, Cabot Cove (from *Murder, She Wrote*), Jaws Lake, and finally Falls Lake, we headed up the hill through the wilderness area and back to the Entertainment Center.

Some may say, "You left out this or that." But remember, back in the early days there wasn't a lot of "this or that." After passing Falls Lake there was nothing but wilderness as we climbed the hill back to the Entertainment Center. As I said, the first few years of the tour we had very few special effects, and they fit the definition of "special effects" only if you are generous.

We were just getting started. But the guests were thrilled to be visiting a working studio. They didn't need the "special things" designed only for the tour. However, to enhance the guest experience we later added the Ice Tunnel, King Kong, Earthquake, Jaws, the Runaway Train, and Battle of Galactica, among others.

In addition to shows in the Entertainment Center, there were also photo ops at the War Lord Tower, (located next to the Woody Woodpecker Theater), an incredible view of the San Fernando Valley (the Entertainment Center was atop the hill overlooking the front and back lots of the studio), and the Snow Set.

The Snow Set was enclosed on three sides with a snowy winter backdrop and the bottom twenty-feet of a fake redwood tree inside. Overhead was a large barrel-shaped-container made of chicken wire and filled with white plastic shavings. Guests could push the button and the drum would spin slowly, causing the "snow" to fall from the chicken-wire barrel, thus creating snow.

The lobby for the tour was eventually moved to another location and the old lobby was turned into a museum. We guides took turns serving as museum curator.

I remember sitting in the museum and, between answering a myriad of questions from the guests, listening to the soundtrack from *Gone with the Wind* playing softly in the background. It played over and over and over ... but I liked the sound track, so the endless loop was okay with me.

At that time I went back to show announcing. The animal and marionette shows were still going strong, but the stunt show moved to a new location in 1970—the amphitheater, with over five-thousand seats. More seats yes, but the amphitheater was a challenging venue for theme park shows because of its size.

The seats in the amphitheater were higher than the stage, even higher than the stunt show high fall. The audience was looking down on the high fall, so it was much less impressive than in the old theater where the audience sat below looking up as the stuntman fell toward them from two stories above. But even with the configuration of the theater, Lance made it work.

The amphitheater had been designed for evening concerts, not for a stunt show. So it was impractical to have a western general store, saloon, and hotel in the background while John Denver, Frank Sinatra, and other artists were performing onstage. The solution was to mount the sets on railroad tracks. Each day after the last stunt show a crew would roll the sets to the side and the amphitheater was magically transformed into a first-class concert venue.

Lance suggested that management come up with an alternative location for the stunt show, just in case something "concert-related" arose that might prevent use of the amphitheater during the day. His suggestion was ignored. Why would that ever arise? Stunt show during the day, concerts in the evening. (Don't get ahead of me. Wait for it.)

Harry Belafonte arrived. Yes, his performances were at night, but he insisted on having the amphitheater all day for rehearsals. Management came to see Lance. "We need to move the stunt show. What do you suggest?" Ever have the urge to say, "I told you so?"

Lance was Lance. He thought for a minute. "How about the old cavalry fort just down the hill from here?"

"That might work. Let's check it out."

They drove to the fort and Lance asked for a few minutes to take in the layout. Then, in a short period of time, he came up with an entire show.

Although the fort wasn't far from the Entertainment Center, it was downhill and along the tram route, so logistically it wasn't feasible for the guests to walk. As a result, the stunt show became part of the guided tour. Three or four trams arrived, the guests disembarked, watched the show, then reboarded the tram and continued the tour. Not the best scenario, but it was a good temporary fix.

Aside from an occasional requirement from a celebrity performer for daytime use of the amphitheater, that venue was the stunt show's home until its permanent theater was completed.

It was while the stunt show was in the Amphitheater that I had to fill in for a stuntman who failed to show up. "Jerry, put on the costume and grab the mic. Show time!" Again, I knew the show so well it was fairly easy.

Fortunately, my part didn't require doing the high fall. That would have crossed a line I wasn't willing to cross. My role as the mic-man was to do what I had seen Lance do so many times; explain to the audience what stuntmen do and how they do it, have a couple of fight scenes, get beaten with a bull whip, shoot the bad guy, and have a polystyrene bottle broken over my head. Piece of cake! That sounds like a lot, and it was, but the show from beginning to end was twelve to thirteen minutes, depending on audience laugh time.

To this day I remember the dialogue from the stunt show. So if Universal calls, I'm ready.

Filling in at the stunt and marionette shows relates back to what I mentioned earlier about being a student of the business. I watched and absorbed everything. Every performance by everyone in every show, even the animal show. Although the opportunity never arose, I think I could have stepped in as the trainer with Benji or Fred the Cockatoo. The only exception to knowing all shows was perhaps the Make-Up Show. Learning that was of no interest for me.

Finances being what they were, I needed a new roommate. I found out that Frankenstein was also looking for a roomy. Enter Richard Annis ... Frankenstein. At least that's the character he played at Universal. He and I became roommates. Richard, nicknamed "Taffy," was an actor who had a re-occurring role in the *Jimmy Stewart Show* sitcom, popular at the time. We had a small two-bedroom apartment on Ventura Boulevard. I never found out how Richard acquired the nickname Taffy.

Taffy told me about an incident when he was strolling through the park interacting with the guests. Our strolling characters like Frankenstein, the Mummy, Woody Woodpecker, and Phantom of the Opera were never supposed to talk. Frankenstein could grunt, but not speak. However, one day an overzealous guest, trying to impress his friends, ran up behind Frankenstein, jumped into the air, and landed on his back, wrapping his arm around his neck. Taffy, a very large guy, reached around and grabbed a handful of hair on the back of the guy's head and jerked him around in front, with the guy's feet dangling in the air. Frankenstein pulled him in so they were nose-to-nose, "If you do that again I'll knock your ******* head off!" Then he shoved the guy away. It was never good when Frankenstein was forced to speak!

Another amusing incident that I recall involved Diane, a tour-guide friend from Montreal. She exited Stage 32 one warm summer day with her group, and since no tram was available, they had to wait in the hub for one to arrive. Trams were backed up, which happened from time to time. As she chatted with the folks in the warm Southern California sun, a sea gull flew over and dropped a large deposit. Splat! Perfect shot! It hit the top of her forehead and stuck. The biggest laugh of the day. But she took it well. Her comment as she looked up, "You might as well, everybody else does." A laugh that big needed to be incorporated into every tour. However, she was *not* onboard with the idea.

A new adventure was just ahead for me. Studio management was about to try something new and asked me to serve as coordinator for the *Robert Q. Lewis Show*, *Ron McCoy Show*, and *Hilly Rose Show* on KFI Radio. Radio? Yep. KFI wanted to do Robert Q's, Ron's, and Hilly's shows in front of a live audience, and Universal had a ready-made audience everyday.

As coordinator, one of my jobs was to invite guests waiting to board the tram to come to the Woody Woodpecker Theatre, watch thirty minutes of radio talk shows, and then return for their tour. It was a fun job. (The Woody Woodpecker Theater was an intimate, cozy little theater that seated about one hundred and twenty, so it was the perfect venue for that type of show.)

I met many, many celebrities while doing the radio shows. Some were very interesting, but after a while they failed to impress—which is not to say I didn't enjoy meeting Charlton Heston, James Garner, and several others. Most were very nice people.

But another celebrity deserves special mention: Art Linkletter.

I usually met the celebs at the front gate of the park and walked them to the theater, as I did with Mr. Linkletter. I always referred to the celebs by their last name unless they gave permission for a first-name connection. That might have something to do with my Southern rearing.

"Good morning, Mr. Linkletter." He responded, "Morning." And that was it. After that there was nothing ... and I mean nothing. He went silent. Really silent. I felt like holding a mirror under his nose to see if he was breathing.

I could understand if he wanted his personal space. He was known the world over, and had at least three television shows, one of them with kids. It wasn't that he seemed angry, but more like his personality had been sucked out.

We walked into the theater where he and Robert Q. exchanged a minimal greeting. He took a seat and readied to go on air. Still nothing. I was standing by with the paddles, just in case.

Five, four, three, two ... Robert Q. could hear "go" in his headset. "We're back. My next guest is someone you all know from *House Party*, *People Are Funny*, and *Kids Say the Darndest Things*, Art Linkletter." (In-studio audience applause.)

It was amazing! I had never witnessed such a transformation. It's like a switch was flipped and Linkletter instantly lit up like a Christmas tree. He was talkative, funny, engaging, personality personified. He could have opened a charm school. Never saw anything like it before or after. It was so dramatic that I remember it above almost everything else related to the radio shows. My take away—have a microphone ready if you want to dialogue with Art.

The Ron McCoy show was easy. He had that easy-going, laid-back attitude. In fact, he wasn't that interested in having an audience. If one was there, okay. If not, okay.

Hilly Rose was a nice man, and although a pioneer in talk radio, he seemed odd. Nice but odd. His show was also easy, and he had the same attitude regarding audiences as Ron McCoy. No audience, no big deal.

But Robert Q. was different. He had a modicum of success as an actor in 1950s and 1960s. But some might have considered him persnickety. Learning early on that he was particular, I made sure I ran his show under his rules.

Since gathering an audience every thirty minutes for the show was a primary part of my job, I wanted to be sure we were clear on one thing. When I arrived with an audience, should I wait for a commercial break before bringing them into the theatre? Robert Q's instructions were, "Bring them in anytime." I made sure that was the correct understanding, and he confirmed it. (Again, you're probably ahead of me.)

To set the stage, the theater had a lobby, and when guests passed through the lobby they entered through the curtained doorway to an area for standing and viewing, kind of a foyer for the actual theater. Beyond that was the theater seating area. The viewing and seating areas were separated by a plate glass wall. There was no audio in the viewing area, so guests could see in, but couldn't hear what was being said.

One day I arrived with an audience while Robert Q. was interviewing a celebrity. I always instructed the guests to be very quiet when entering, so we tip-toed in. Halfway in Robert Q. threw out his hand toward us several times, dictator style, like he was ready to come over the table after me. (Robert Q. was a little scrawny guy and I was fresh out of the Army, so I'm pretty sure I could have taken him.) I whipped around and whispered to the group to wait.

Having just entered the theater, we didn't know that the guest celebrity was telling the radio audience about a tragic event in his life, the death of a child. Had we known, of course we would have waited before entering.

At the commercial break, Robert Q. began to unload on me in front of the celebrity and the in-studio audience; the same audience I just brought in to be entertained by his wit and wisdom. Remember that short fuse I mentioned earlier that I had when I was younger. Boom! It was lit! However, I did wait until the audience left for the tour. But then....

Robert Q. and I were separated only because he was on one side of the table and I was on the other. His final comment, "Maybe I'll go to the office and tell them about this!"

I was in his face. "Do you need directions, or can you get there on your own!"

I will say, even though Robert Q. and I had conflicting personalities, except for that one incident, we always got along very well. He even invited me to his home for his annual Christmas party. For the record, he never went to the office, and we both forgot about the "kerfuffle," as Judge Judy might call it.

After several months KFI pulled the plug on all three shows. By that time park attendance had slowed so the need for a large number of guides also diminished. So back to the question—what to do with Jerry?

How about the wardrobe department? Wardrobe? Yes, I was assigned to wardrobe. No, not sewing clothes, but handing out costumes to Frankenstein, Woody Woodpecker, tour guides, stuntmen, and other performers. It wasn't the job of my dreams, but I was still part of the team. I could do it.

I spent about three months in the wardrobe department. Then one day Cliff Walker, operations manager, came to me. I remember the conversation because that moment was going to have a profound impact on the rest of my life. "Jerry, I know working in wardrobe isn't what you want to do, but I appreciate your attitude. I'm gonna move you to Stage 70." I remember Cliff talking about *attitude* and *moving me to a show.* Stage 70! WOW!

Stage 70 was an open audition for every guest who wanted their fifteen minutes of fame. The show, which later became known as Screen Test Comedy Theater, was just that.

The show gave anyone from anywhere a chance to perform. How? Prior to the show the crew went into the park and found fifteen to eighteen guests who wanted to be a "stars." They were given costumes, then rehearsed in scenes from the movie or television show on which our live stage show was based.

After re-creating the scenes with our guest actors on stage in front of a live audience, the technical director intercut/edited their performance with actual scenes from the original movie or television show. So our finished "movie" made it look as if the guests were in the original movie or TV show along with the stars from that production. Then the completed show was played back on closed circuit TVs in the theater.

Stage 70's first show was a spoof on Western movies—not very sophisticated, and short lived. I was still in the Army when this began, but I was told that tour guides were assigned to do the show. This was all new stuff. We were making it up as we went.

The second show was based on the original movie *Airport*, with Burt Lancaster, Dean Martin, and George Kennedy. With the new show we took a step toward sophistication. Tech people with advanced degrees were hired from Columbia College, and hosts had to audition for the job. Enter Don Martin, Bob Formica, Larry Curran, and Ken Smedley.

Don was the technical director (TD), Bob was cameraman and part-time TD, and Larry and Ken each shared hosting responsibilities. Everyone learned the job of cameraman to allow for days off.

The show was budgeted for only one camera man, yet it was a two-camera show. So how did that work? One camera was locked in a wide shot and left unattended, while the second camera was manned for close-ups and to follow the action. It wasn't until more than fifteen years later that the budget was increased to two cameramen per show.

The Stage 70 theater was small, seating approximately eight hundred, and the stage itself was perhaps thirty-five feet across. During its *Airport* days, it consisted of a mockup of an airplane cockpit, the interior of a small part of the fuselage, and a portion of the bathroom where Van Heflin detonated his briefcase bomb.

When I came on board at Stage 70, the show was based on the popular television series *Adam-12*, starring Martin Milner and Kent McCord, and created by Jack Webb and R.A. Cinader. The TV show ran for seven seasons. The live stage show based on *Adam-12* had a well-oiled crew of four when I arrived and had been going for about a year. So would I fit in? Time would tell.

How did an opening at the show come to be? Entrepreneurship is the answer.

The most frequently asked question by those guests who participated in the show was, "Can we get a copy to take home and show our friends?" Of course that wasn't something the studio had planned for, so the answer was, "Sorry, no-can-do."

However, Don and Ken, being the greedy little entrepreneurs they were (at least that's what we called them), had a brilliant idea. "Let's start a company, a concession, and sell copies of the show on 16mm film." (Cassettes would come later.) They pitched the idea and Universal gave the green light. They were off and running.

Their business venture proved to be very successful. Ken quit his position as host/director and devoted full time to the new venture, but Don remained as technical director. He and Ken hired cameramen, independent of the Stage 70 crew employed by Universal, to film the show and sell copies afterward. Al Gries, Gary Zietlow, Ahmed Tuck, and Wilson Farragut were brought in to fill the role.

Don lasted longer at Universal than any of us—forty years. He was always eager to learn new things—computers when they first came on market, he learned to be a locksmith, he built his own one-seater airplane from a kit, and he learned pyrotechnics. In later years, when shows in the park evolved to include more sophisticated special effects, Don worked as manager in charge of pyro.

But with Ken's departure from the show that opened the door for another director—me. As I mentioned earlier, the microphone person in the show was called the "director." The reason was to make the show sound more like a production crew. We had a technical director, cameraman, and director. The director's role, under different circumstances, would be thought of as an emcee or host or master of ceremonies. In any event he was the one doing all the talking.

Shortly after my arrival at Stage 70, Larry, Bob, and I began a concession of our own. Guests could sit in the Adam-12 car and have their picture taken for a fee. I can't remember what the charge was, but we made good money until we moved to a new theater. Of course guests could use their own camera without paying the fee, but most were anxious to pay just to be in the Adam-12 car.

As I said, the Stage 70 theater seated about eight hundred, and was built in such a way as to create an intimate feel. The last row was about forty feet from the stage. The first row of the audience was the same level as the stage, and there was no separation between the audience and the stage except a thin rail. So the audience was toe-to-toe with the performers, and from a performer's perspective, it was the perfect theater.

I walked into my new home ready to learn hosting/directing. I soon discovered that directing shows was in some ways the same as giving tours, but in many ways different; in some ways more challenging, and less in others.

Tour guiding gave me an hour and a half with the guests. Stage 70 was twenty to twenty-five minutes from beginning to end. And although the theater was an intimate setting, tour guiding allowed me to mingle with the group as we moved through the sound stages. The show was different in that respect. It was here that I learned about *crowd mentality*.

(A disclaimer – the following is *jerryosophy*, and not to be confused with scientific research. It's an understanding of audiences I learned during my career of directing/hosting over 32,000 live shows.)

Audiences develop a mentality depending on the seating configuration. When seated in a tram, five across, one row behind the other, each person's experience is more individualized. And although they may hear the person in front or behind laughing, there's a feeling of segregation. There's less camaraderie because the interaction is hindered.

But, put the crowd in a common area, such as a theater like Stage 70, and voilà, that feeling of community quickly develops as they take on a "group mentality." Their experience becomes a "shared" experience.

Also, the design of the theater impacts the audience. Stage 70 was perfect for interaction and developing audience rapport. A couple of years later we moved our show to a theater that was designed differently, and it changed the audience dynamic. Trust me, not all architects understand the concept.

(By the way, crowd or group mentality can be channeled in the wrong direction. For proof, catch the evening news.)

Although I learned the following later when we moved to another venue, I'll share it here since I'm talking about the audience mentality.

Our goal was always to start shows on time; however, occasional delays were unavoidable. Technical or mechanical malfunctions happen. But I learned another aspect of crowd mentality after experiencing the first couple of show delays.

Audiences usually allow a five-minute delay without much concern. But after ten minutes they get antsy. A couple minutes more and someone in the crowd would usually begin clapping, then a few more would start, and then the entire audience would join in, wanting us to get it started. Finally, after correcting the problem, I would step on stage and welcome everyone and apologize for the delay.

Was the crowd angry? Was the show a disaster because of the delay? On the contrary. A dynamic was created during the delay that was most interesting.

The delays that generated the collective audience clapping were always the best of the day. Why? As the clapping began, with one person at first, then swept across the audience to encompass everyone, a sense of community developed as they worked together toward a common goal.

Rather than two thousand individuals watching a show, they became one entity; many functioning as one. For the remainder of the show they laughed as one and applauded as one. What one thought was funny, everyone thought was funny. And although I hated delays, I found that to be true *every* time we experienced one.

I spent a couple of days watching the show, learning the audio cues, what the "actors" from the audience should be doing, and when and where to do it. I learned to cue the actors so their movements and dialogue matched those previously recorded by Martin Milner and Kent McCord. And after a couple of days, it was time to take the leap.

Bob Formica, the cameraman, handed me the microphone. I took a deep breath, walked on stage in front of eight hundred people, and said, "Good afternoon, ladies and gentlemen, welcome to Stage 70...." We were underway and all eyes were on me, including the crew, waiting to see how the new guy would do. I remember staying close to Bob during that first show, so he could quietly prompt me on cues that I might have otherwise missed. As was true in giving tours, practicing was different from performing.

One of the most difficult parts of writing my story of twenty-five years at Universal is to accurately describe for you Bob Formica. I can't. He was a most unique individual—a combination of General Patton, Henny Youngman, and a third element that can't be described. He was Bob! Indelibly imprinted on the hearts of everyone at the show. (I always called him Formica.)

Formica would often make comments into the headset that only the crew could hear. I didn't wear a headset so he would wait until I passed by then make the comment to try and get me to crack while I was talking to the audience.

In today's overly sensitive society some would consider his comments out of line, judgmental, or even racist. He might see a group of priests from Nepal sitting in the audience wearing their traditional long robes, and say, "Call the Sheraton and tell them somebody took their sheets." Or if Sikhs were there wearing turbans, he would say, "Call the Sheraton. I found their towels." Bob wasn't prejudiced. That was his sense of humor.

When the Screen Test shows closed many years later, Bob went to work for Boulder Station Casinos in Las Vegas as their entertainment manger.

Anyway, I got through the first show and the audience was entertained, but equally important the crew accepted me as part of the pack. So the revised team at Stage 70 became Don, Larry, Bob, and me. A year or so later another person would join us—Joe Turpel. Good guy. And with the addition of Joe, the nucleus was intact for the next fifteen years, until I transitioned into management.

(Not long after I joined the show we changed the casting process, and made it a part of the show. The director would cast guests from the audience about twenty minutes prior to the official start of the show.)

I continued to refine my hosting skills, and Stage 70 was the perfect place to do it. It was easier to get laughs and feedback from the audience in that environment. The theater was small enough that if someone in the last row made a comment, everyone could hear it. And, because the show was "audience participation," they were inclined to make comments when given the chance.

When time permitted I would go on stage ten or fifteen minutes before casting and do a Q&A with the audience. "We have a few minutes before the show starts, and I'd be happy to answer any questions you might have. Ask me anything," I would tell them. And they did. They had the opportunity to ask questions that might not have been answered on the guided tour. It usually turned out to be great fun. It wasn't something management required or even asked me to do. I did it because I loved my job.

The chemistry between the audience and me in that pre-show Q&A made the show that much better. We talked and laughed so much it was sometimes disappointing to have to stop and do a show.

I remember one evening, the last show of the day around 7:40, I was talking and joking with the audience before the show. The crowd always liked it when someone from their side took me on with lively banter. Enter their hero—a lady with a great sense of humor was sitting in the back and began asking questions and making comments, not heckling ... just a funny back-and-forth with me for several minutes. It almost turned into her own show. I let her go on for a while, getting in several good jabs, and then I paused and asked, "Didn't I see you last night on Hollywood Boulevard, asking some guy, 'Hey sailor, new in town?'" I knew it was a Don Rickles line, but it fit the moment. The audience laughed, but more importantly, the lady laughed. That humor, telling a lady she had loose morals in front of eight hundred people, would not have worked without first getting to know her and my audience.

You say, "That kind of humor works all the time for Rickles. So what's the big deal?" The difference is, Rickles' audiences go to see him knowing what they're getting. If he didn't do that kind of humor they would be disappointed. Folks came to Stage 70 with no preconceived idea of content. But after spending ten minutes visiting with them, I knew I could get away with it. The same joke might not have worked for a show earlier in the day. But the evening crowd was a different dynamic.

Another time during the preshow Q&A I answered a question asked by an audience member and then, trying not to sound like a know-it-all, I followed it with, "But what do I know?" Someone from the back of the audience yelled, "Nothing!" His timing was perfect and so, a big laugh.

After we completed filming the show (although we didn't use film, but instead video tape), we took a couple of minutes to briefly interview four or five people who had the biggest parts in our little production. That gave Don, the TD, time to get the completed video ready for playback. As I talked with one lady about her life "outside of show biz," she told the audience about her job in the corporate world. It was an important position and impressive to say the least. After she finished I couldn't let the opportunity pass, so I said, "I thought women were supposed to be housewives, stay home, have babies, and cook." A mix of boos and laughs from the audience followed. But everyone understood I made the joke because of her impressive résumé. She laughed, too. (When Don heard I was writing about my years at the studio, he reminded me to be sure to retell that incident. It stuck with him.) Remember, the women's lib movement was in full swing at the time. My comment, meant as a joke, might not be taken the same way today, when everyone is looking for ways to be offended. Back then people could laugh at themselves, and each other, without feeling "repressed."

Our show was different from other shows, like the stunt show, for example. That show had three performers per show and Lance made sure every show was the same. Lines delivered the same, timing the same, and so forth. The Stage 70 Show was three men on stage, but only one person had a microphone, and that belonged to me (aside from the TD saying over his microphone, "We're rolling," and "Speed." Speed meant the sound and film were synced together, although we weren't using film. Remember, things were done and said to make it look and sound like an actual production of a movie or TV show.) But I was free to say anything or change the pace of every show if I wanted.

As long as we finished the show in the allotted time, it was at the director's discretion on how to get there. Larry and I, and eventually Joe, had our own style of getting to the finish line. If we got too far off course, the crew reeled us back in after the show.

After a few months at Stage 70 Terry asked me to be show captain. It was my responsibility to represent the crew to management, schedule personnel, and ensure that all shows started on time and ended reasonably on time. If a show went long it could affect guests getting from our show to the next scheduled show in the park, perhaps the stunt show or the animal show.

But to be honest, our show ran itself. All the guys knew their job extremely well, worked the same days every week for fifteen years, and had the same days off. Things rarely changed. I had Sundays and Thursdays off. Why split? Because when I joined the team I was lowest in the food chain, and that's what was available. So as the years passed I kept the same days off because I grew used to it.

In November 1974, another momentous event happened in my life, I met a young lady named Pam. She was pretty, sweet, and a gentle, non-show biz lady who had a cute, sweet six-year-old daughter named Susie (now spelled Suzi—like Kimi, I guess it's cooler).

Truth be known, Pam didn't really like me at first. (Perhaps I'm being presumptuous in assuming she does now.) But one evening I was hosting a non-Universal talent show with another friend, Earl Robinson. Pam and Suzi sang a duet as part of the show. As their song concluded I made a few complimentary remarks about her in front of the audience. Her best friend, Grace, nudged her and said, "He's the one."

We began dating in February and early in our relationship I invited her to lunch at the Universal commissary. I was sure that would score points for me. And it worked.

She loved it! She was impressed because she got to be around her most favorite hunk, her dreamboat. No, not me. James Garner! He was having lunch there also. (It's one of the few times I've seen her drool.) Fortunately, he was married at the time, so I still stood a chance.

On another occasion I took her to the commissary, and that time we saw Charlton Heston. Another guy who was already married, so I was still in the running. Having access to the commissary paid off because it was a good place to find celebs.

We married in September 1975, six months after our first date, by Grace's future husband, Tom Halstead. Tom became a lifelong friend; even to this day he continues to play a significant role in my life. Several years after Grace passed away, Tom married a lovely lady named Shahry. They are still good friends with Pam and me.

On the day of our wedding, the last Stage 70 show was scheduled for 7:40, and no, I didn't have to work. But Terry changed the schedule and moved our show earlier in the last rotation of shows so the crew could attend the wedding.

Do you think they would come to the wedding as normal, well-dressed human beings? Or course not! They came wearing costumes from the show we were doing at the time, Emergency. Larry came dressed as a doctor, Bob as a fireman, and Joe as a paramedic. I can't remember what Don was dressed as.

In the mid-seventies we moved from Stage 70 to our new theater across the park, the Screen Test Theater. Our venue went from seating eight hundred people and a twenty-minute show, to seating 2,000 people and a forty-minute show.

Like Stage 70, the theater was open air. But where Stage 70 had a green awning to provide shade, Screen Test had none. We basked in the warm, sometimes blistering, southern California sun. (An awning would soon be added.)

Our new stage was ninety feet across and perhaps thirty feet deep. The technical director's booth at Stage 70 was ground level, tucked around on the side of the stage, almost hidden. The booth for the new and improved Screen Test Theater was a plate-glass enclosure located above the stage. The audience could now watch Don edit the show as it took place—but not really. That was the idea, but it was too difficult to see the small monitors from the audience, and with his back turned, the detail of his job was lost. Not to mention, everyone was watching their friends and family perform on stage. But it made Don feel like he was a more visual part of the team, so we let him believe the audience was watching. I could do more sarcastic jokes here, but won't.

Behind the stage was a plethora of dressing rooms where the guests could change into costumes, plus a break room for the crew to relax between shows.

Two of our four sets included the front half of a paramedic's truck and a fake brick wall with two windows that were five feet off the stage. We filmed the window scenes in such a way to make it look as if they were two stories up. Creative editing would make that seem real. One window was where a guest actor, playing the role of a paramedic, climbed a ladder to rescue a trapped person from a burning building, and the second window was, of course, for our fire effect. Yes, real fire. We always kidded that Disneyland used fake fire—cellophane, lights, and wind to create the illusion of fire. Not us! We had real fire. It was the little things that mattered.

A third set was the interior of an emergency room, and a fourth was the exterior of a building with a real police car. On the ground near the police car was a small puddle with a special effect that created the appearance of bullets hitting the water.

How did the Screen Test crew work together so successfully for so many years?

The break room was the key. That room made our friendship work. Only the passing of Larry and Formica interrupted the relationship. As of this writing Don, Joe, and I are still alive. (Some might argue the point, but yes, I'm still here.) Larry passed away from the results of a stroke, and Formica from a brain tumor.

So how did the break room prolong the relationship? Blood lettings. That's what we called them, blood letting. Only crew members were allowed in these blood lettings— no stage hands, no management, no one except the crew.

So what's a blood letting? Simple. We would go into the break room, spread out so that no one was right next to you, take a seat, then turn off the lights. When the lights were off you couldn't see your hand in front of your face; even after half-an-hour it was still pitch black.

With the lights off, everyone could say what was on their mind about anyone else on the crew. Anything that was bothering you could be said, and no one could respond until it was his turn. When your turn came, you could explain something that perhaps the other person had misunderstood, and/or voice your own grievances. Although there was no time limit, the blood lettings rarely lasted more than forty minutes.

But it's amazing how well it worked. It was extremely effective. With the lights off it seemed much easier to give and take criticism. No one could see anyone else. No one was offended.

I am convinced the "sharing time" (it's a nicer way of saying blood lettings) was the key to our friendship that lasted so many years. We truly cared for each other— to this day Don, Joe, and I stay in touch via text and FaceBook, and an occasional lunch.

Several years ago Larry suffered a severe stroke which robbed him of his ability to walk and talk. I remember visiting him from time-to-time in the convalescent home in Orange County. In addition to not being able to talk, his wife said he rarely expressed emotion. But when I visited and relived some of the Screen Test stories with him, he would laugh so hard that once we had to call the nurse to help calm him down.

After he moved to Las Vegas, Formica would call me or I called him from time to time. The conversation always began the same way, and depending on who was calling whom, the first line was usually, "Hey stupid, get to the phone faster next time. Don't make me wait." If I started the conversation, there would always be a welcomed greeting in his voice, "Hey Greenie!" He always called me Greenie.

Formica was the picture of health. He worked out regularly, took vitamins, did all those things we're supposed to do to stay healthy. Then one day a fellow casino employee saw Formica sitting by himself with a confused look on his face. He asked, "Are you okay?" Formica replied, "I don't know where I am or how I got here." That was the beginning of the end for Bob, as the brain tumor progressed rapidly.

Formica was ever the prankster. He told me that one day he was visiting his chiropractor, who was also a good friend of his. They worked out together at the gym. After a brief time in the exam room receiving an adjustment, his friend the chiropractor told him to wait there and he'd be right back. So Formica, being Formica, decided to take off all his clothes and stand on a chair while posing like a Greek god. Kind of the Schwarzenegger pose. A moment later the door opened and the doctor reappeared. "Hey Bob, I want you to meet Burt ... Reynolds...." He and Burt looked up to see Formica standing naked on the chair and posing. "Uh, never mind," the doctor said as he and Reynolds backed out and closed the door. Formica climbed off the chair, got dressed and quietly slipped out, having missed the chance to meet the number-one box-office star in the world.

Another time Formica took a young lady on a first date to a restaurant for dinner. He asked the waitress if he could get a lobster, but he wanted to see it before it was cooked.

Moments later the waitress appeared at the table with the lobster. He took a string and tied it around the little guy, then took it outside, and set it free. (I think he took it back in before it died.)

Another time, while dining at an Italian restaurant with management from the studio, Formica excused himself and went to the restroom. A few minutes later he returned wearing a toilet seat cover around his neck with the flap pulled down like a bib. He sat down at the table as if nothing was out of the ordinary.

Still another time, Formica was leaving the park at the same time as Lance. They decided to grab dinner together, so Lance followed him in his car down the hill. About half-way down Formica hit his brakes, drove into the curb, and rolled out of his car onto the pavement as if having a heart attack. Lance saw him and thought Bob was dying, so he jumped from his car and raced toward him. When Lance got close, Formica got up, casually stepped back into his car, and drove off, leaving Lance standing in the middle of the street.

Lance got back in his car and caught up with him at a restaurant in Toluca Lake, a place that was a frequent hangout for Formica. When dinner was just about over, Formica told Lance he had to go to the restroom. After about ten minutes Lance became worried, thinking that maybe Formica really did have a heart attack in the men's room, so he asked the waitress, "Have you seen Bob?"

"Oh, yeah, he left about ten minutes ago," she replied.

Lance got stuck with the bill.

There are enough Formica stories for a book of his own. He was his own category.

One night we closed Stage 70 and the next morning we opened in the new venue. The theme of the new show—*Emergency*. It was based on the TV show of the same name starring Kevin Tighe and Randy Mantooth.

Another program created by Jack Webb, R.A. Cinader, and Harold Bloom.

Our Emergency was an entertaining show. The audience could relate because they watched it every week on television. Terry produced the show, meaning he designed the physical stage and sets, but he depended on us to come up with content, and we usually did that by trial and error.

Earlier in the story I emphasize the importance of viewing the show from the audience's perspective. The configuration of our new stage provides a perfect example.

If you recall, the technical director's booth was just above the stage and visible to the audience through the plate-glass window. One day, just as I closed the show, I turned and looked at the booth. The TD was standing in front of the glass, in full view of the audience, making gestures with his thumb pointing down. Kind of like a hitchhiker's motion, except rather than moving side-to-side with his thumb, his motion was up-and-down.

I knew what he wanted—to remind us to turn off the fire effect in the window I described earlier. But what do you think the audience thought he might be referring to? The quality of the show. To them the TD was saying the show stunk! An important member of the crew was gesturing in a downward motion with his thumb just as the show ended. Gulp! Innocence in the TD's mind, but an editorial from the audience's perspective. Evaluating from the right perspective is important.

I always enjoyed playing off what was happening on stage. If an audience participant was a "ham," I would use that. If the crew messed up, I would use that. Sometimes I even orchestrated situations on the fly.

I remember once while interviewing guests at the end of the show, I came to the young lady last in line. She was wearing a T-shirt that had written across the front "I'm with stupid," and just below the wording was an arrow pointing to the right. Joe was busy behind us doing what he always did when the show ended, putting away equipment and getting ready for the next show. I called him on the microphone, "Joe, would you join us over here for a sec?" He looked confused because there was no logical reason for me to call him. He was busy.

I didn't explain to the audience what I was doing. But when Joe walked over I took him by the arm and positioned him to the right of the young lady wearing the T-shirt. He stood there for only a second before the audience caught on and began laughing. Joe was still clueless. As the laughter grew he began looking around, first behind him, then side to side. When he didn't see anything that looked out of place, he just stood there thinking they were laughing at something unrelated to him. But after a few more seconds he began looking around again, and finally caught sight of the woman's shirt. He played the moment perfectly, as if we rehearsed it, which of course we hadn't. When he caught on to the joke the laughter grew really loud. He gave an "I've been had" look to the audience. They loved it. Again, the audience always enjoyed seeing one of us being *had*, and Joe was probably the best I ever saw at playing that part when the opportunity presented itself.

Our show was so popular, and the concept so good, that Universal created a version for TV called *Don Adams' Screen Test*. From my way of thinking it could have just as easily been Jerry Green's Screen Test. What's wrong with that? Oh, that's right. I wasn't a household name. I never had a successful TV show called *Get Smart!* A minor detail.

The Mike Douglas Show was one of the first afternoon talk/variety shows on television, and ran for over twenty years. Every name in Hollywood eventually made their way to his show. And now Mike was bringing his show to southern California and wanted to visit the Screen Test Theater.

When he arrived he was not content to just watch the show, he wanted to participate. Who knows, perhaps it was his producers who wanted him to do it, but regardless, he was game.

After much discussion it was decided that the role of the "policeman" would fit Mike perfectly. He donned the police uniform, we rehearsed a bit and then ... show time. Not only was Mike willing to do whatever we asked, he was anxious to do it and threw himself into the role.

His part started with him and other police officers pinned down behind a car, being fired at by a sniper across the street. He was to run across the stage, get shot, and fall next to the water effect mid-stage. I cued him, he started running, and at the precise moment he reacted to the sniper's bullet. But do you think he just dropped like the scene called for? Of course not. He took the hit, spun around, wobbled, spun around again, stopped and waved at the camera, spun again, gave an "okay" sign to the audience, then gingerly fell to the stage floor, and continued jiggling his body from time to time.

As he lay next to the special-effect puddle, bullet hits continued to strike the water next to him. He raised up, waved at the camera, then leaned over and scooped up a handful of the water from the puddle and drank it. Yuck! I yelled into the microphone for him not to drink it, but his adrenaline was pumping and he gulped it down, looked up at the audience and gave another "okay" sign, then lay back. I yelled, "Cut!"

The water in the little puddle wasn't filtered, and we never replaced it with clean water. It just occupied that little puddle, three feet across, in the hot California sun day after day, week after week. The last thing we ever expected was for someone to drink it. To the best of our knowledge he never got sick from the puddle water.

Mike was a great guest and the audience really enjoyed watching him get into the part. It was also a thrill for the guest actors from the audience to participate in the show with him, then to see their performance on national television on *The Mike Douglas Show* a few weeks later.

In 1978, it was time for a new show at the Screen Test Theater. Emergency had served its purpose and put us on par with the other shows. We were no longer the ugly stephild.

What would be our next theme? One of our earlier stage shows, Airport, had done well at Stage 70. The movie was very popular, grossing over $100,000,000 in 1970. That's $600,000,000 in 2016 dollars. So, how about another airplane disaster movie? *Airport '77*, the sequel to the sequel (*Airport '75* was sandwiched in-between) didn't do as well at the box office, pulling in $30,000,000 on a budget of $6,000,000. It was still a respectable number—$120,000,000 in today's dollars.

But truth be known, as would prove true by the show that followed Airport '77, we really didn't need a specific movie or TV show to make a good Screen Test production.

So *Airport '77* was the film on which we'd base the new show. The movie at least had plenty of star power, including Jack Lemmon, James Stewart, George Kennedy, Joseph Cotton, Brenda Vacarro, Lee Grant, and Christopher Lee.

Of course, oversight of the show fell to Terry. But while he was taking care of construction, our team got busy with content. It should be understood that the difference in set construction between Emergency and Airport '77 was the difference between night and day. Emergency was a stage with five small, simple sets—two flat walls, plus part of a fire truck, a paramedic truck, and a police car. That was it.

The sets for Airport '77 included a first-class section of a private 747 fuselage, a cockpit, a giant wing extending from the side of the plane into the audience (used as a ramp leading onto the stage), and a six-thousand-gallon tank where guests would leap from a cockpit door into the water. The water tank was made of three-inch-thick glass on the two sides that faced the audience.

To add to Terry's degree of difficulty, the side of the 747 lifted to reveal the passengers inside (guest actors from the audience), plus the cabin was mounted on a gimbal controlled by hydraulics. Using a knob on the control panel that I operated on stage during the show, I could make the plane appear to be flying out of control, rocking and rolling and tossing people around in the cabin.

In determining content, our first job was to edit a one-hundred-thirteen-minute movie down to seven minutes, and still tell a coherent story. That was not a task for the faint-hearted. We arranged with the editing department on the lower lot for an editor, and they sent us Bill Parker. Bill was another good guy, and an excellent editor, whose primarily responsibility was editing the *Emergency* TV show.

On day one, Don, Larry, Bob, Joe, and I went to Bill's edit bay on the lower lot where he cued up the film on his Moviola. It didn't take long to discover, but editing by committee was going to be a disaster. One of the guys would suggest an edit, Bill would make the cut, then someone would object to the way it looked. After an hour or so Bill was ready to pull out his hair. He pulled me aside, "Jerry, this isn't good." I agreed.

"Guys, we have to rethink our strategy," I told them. The decision was made that I would continue editing and they would go back to the Entertainment Center. Now that I think of it, what were they doing all that time while I was editing?

Anyhow, after a couple of weeks we had our seven-minute show that told the same story as the hundred-and-thirteen-minute film, except ours allowed for guests from the audience to play some of the roles.

A brief movie synopsis will help you understand the stage show. A private 747 owned by Jimmy Stewart's character was flying his guests and valuable pieces of art to his island for a special event. The plane was hijacked, then crashed into the Atlantic Ocean and sank, coming to rest on sandbar deep enough to cover the plane, but leaving the top of the tail above water. The only way to alert the Navy to their location was for someone (Christopher Lee's character) to open the cargo hold and swim to the surface and set off a beacon. What happens if you open the door to an empty room while underwater? The entire Atlantic Ocean rushes in, instantly! Keep that thought in mind.

Opening day isn't just a day that you shoot for and if you don't make it, just open a week or two later. It's a drop-dead day. Celebrities were scheduled to attend, the press was invited, and the bosses' bosses were coming—Lew Wasserman, Sid Sheinberg, Jay Stein, and celebrities like Jimmy Stewart. It was a *big* day!

However, we were not on schedule. Things were running behind as the tech and construction crews worked with a myriad of contractors, doing things never done before, and doing them in a way that allowed guests to have a good time without putting their lives in danger.

The tank was located stage right. It held six-thousand gallons of water, and was unproven and untested. The first scene began with the tank dry, as the Christopher Lee character pretended to open a side door in the cargo hold of the plane. Remember my mention of the Atlantic Ocean flooding the empty room? Well, when the door was opened, the room flooded—instantly.

How did we accomplish that on stage? It isn't like using a garden hose or even a fire hose to fill it. It has to fill almost *instantly*. The solution was to build an elevated tank behind the theater, twenty-five feet in the air. When I pushed the "flood button" on my console on stage, the floor of the tank behind the stage dropped open and the water rushed up through a steel grate in the floor of the tank. The tank went from dry to flooded in two or three seconds.

As we were readying to start the first show I heard one of the techs ask, "Do you think the force of the water will shoot whoever's in there out the top?" The truth is, we didn't know.

The second use of the tank was to replicate a small part of the Atlantic Ocean. At the end of the movie Jack Lemmon and Brenda Vaccaro rushed up the stairs and jumped into the ocean as the plane was going down for the second time. We wanted to replicate that scene in our show.

Not being ready on opening day is the kind of scenario you want to avoid, but this was in the days before "soft openings." We only knew *hard* openings. So, how did ours go?

The morning was drawing to a close and noon was approaching. Everyone was rushing around verifying that all bolts were tightened, clamps secured on the hydraulic lines, that the three-inch-thick glass in the tank was anchored and sealed properly, and so on.

Meanwhile, the show crew and I were waiting. We had done all we could do, which was to *think* about the show, and discuss the shots we wanted, because up to that point we didn't have access to the stage for rehearsals. We had a pretty good idea of the shots we needed, but hadn't done any blocking. I knew the order of the scenes and where I wanted to go with the narration. But the details had to be worked out in rehearsal, which we never had.

As noon passed and one o'clock approached, Terry and I were standing on stage next to the water tank, the effect that had everyone nervous. We watched as the maintenance men double-checked the bolts holding the grate, which served as the floor of the tank.

The theater was packed, and with no curtain to block their view, the audience could see we were scrambling. Terry looked at the theater filled to capacity, then looked at me and said, "Jerry, everybody's here. We have to do a show."

"Okay, let's do a show." I told him we would cast all the parts except the two that took place in the tank. We would cut that scene to one person and use a maintenance guy as the actor. "They're expendable," I joked.

(I think the maintenance man's name was Chuck, but I'm not sure. He deserves an honorable mention. I do remember he eagerly volunteered. He must have had a secret desire to be a stuntman, or had a death wish.)

So, with no rehearsal I picked up the microphone and walked to the edge of the stage, smiled at the two-thousand plus fans, media, managers, and celebrities, and began, "Good afternoon, ladies and gentlemen. Welcome to the new Screen Test Theater." I explained that it was our first show and they were getting a behind-the-scenes look as we took thirty-five guests from the audience and made them into movie stars in our production of Airport '77.

And with that we were off and running as I cast thirty-plus people from the audience. Our first show took longer than we wanted, but the audience enjoyed taking that journey with us. We received excellent publicity and the show ran until we replaced it with The Great Chase some years later. Visually, it was an impressive show with the airplane rocking and rolling center stage and the water tank providing all kinds of fun.

It was a warm summer day. We were doing multiple shows—twelve to fourteen each day, and probably a year and a half into the Airport '77 run. By this time we had the show down to thirty-five minutes, including casting and the seven-minute playback of the completed video at the end.

We were rolling along during an afternoon show and got to the water tank scene. Our guest "actors," a man and a woman, were in the tank and taking their roles very seriously, as most of the guests did. He was pretending to struggle with the door handle, as if trying to open the cargo hold. The woman was close beside, encouraging him on. Good so far. I was calling out instructions to them on the microphone: "Keep struggling with the handle. The lives of everyone on the plane depend on you getting that door open."

Remember, in the tank you were dry one moment, then two or three seconds later the water was over your head. It's one thing to tell people about it, but another to actually experience it.

I hit the console button. Whoosh! The tank was instantly flooded, and even though the man had been briefed on what was going to happen, he was shocked, as was the lady. They floated around for a couple of seconds until we got the shot we needed.

"And cut!" I said over the microphone. The audience applauded and I hit the console button to drain the water from the tank. Keep in mind, the water drained just as quickly as it entered. So the tank was suddenly empty of water. I told our guest actors they could exit through the door on the side of the tank. It was a door similar to that in a submarine.

The lady started toward the door, but the man was bent slightly at the waist with his back to the audience, as if looking for something. I asked him, "Sir, is everything okay? Did you lose something?" Even though we provided a complete change of wardrobe, occasionally folks carried personal belongings with them rather than leave them in their dressing room, which we also provided.

I asked him again, "Did you lose something?"

He mumbled back, and I thought I heard him say, "I lost my keys."

I asked, "You lost your keys? You took your keys in the tank with you?!"

He turned and faced the two-thousand-person audience, and with a big grin pointed to his mouth, "No, I lost my teeth!"

The roar of laughter that erupted from the audience numbed the ears. They went crazy! People were coming out of their seats. And it continued and continued. The laughter went on for five minutes. People from outside the open-air theater were trying to get in to see what was going.

I know, five minutes sounds like an exaggerated time. No laugh goes on for five minutes. But it went on and on until we had to temporarily stop the show. It was impossible to continue. The audience and the crew were hysterical. The man just stood there with a big toothless grin.

It was, without a doubt, the longest stage laugh I ever heard, and as I said, I hosted a lot of shows.

So how did he lose his teeth? When the water flooded the tank he was so startled that he opened his mouth to gasp and his teeth floated out. Then before he could grab them, I hit the button and his teeth, along with the water, headed for the drain. As he later explained, he was grabbing for them, but with no success.

Fortunately, a wire on his dentures caught and was dangling on the underside of the floor grate, so we were able to retrieve them. If the teeth had made it past the grate it would have required a diver to go into the reservoir behind the stage to find them. (For you germaphobes like me, the water was cleaned and recycled after each use. At least that's what we told the guests. No, actually it was sanitized each time.)

Formica, the cameraman, wanted to have a chance at hosting the show. But then so did everybody. Even though most of the crew expressed interest in hosting, only three put effort into learning how to do it.

I told Formica we would work on it for a while and see. We did. Honest, we worked on it. I remembered back to my tour guide training and how someone gave me a chance when I probably wasn't ready.

After a while he began to show progress and I decided to give him a shot. Maybe he'll relax more when he gets into it. He was a funny guy ... as proven by the "Formica stories" told earlier. (In Formica's defense, he was the first person I ever trained to host.)

On that summer day he was nervous, but he picked up the microphone and walked to the front of the stage and began with a drill-sergeant-tone, "Okay, listen up, you people...." And that was as good as it got. It went downhill after that. Might I suggest for those wanna-be show hosts, never begin with, "Okay, listen up, you people."

You've heard of stage freight? Formica had a variation of that. He had microphone fright. Being in front of the audience didn't bother him, he had done that for years. But with a microphone in his hand, his mind froze. He was one of those people who was hysterically funny until he was standing in front of an audience with a mic.

Frankly, if he hadn't been "one of the guys," he would never had gotten the chance in the first place. He was a very good cameraman and a fairly good TD, but hosting wasn't in his arsenal. I did give him another shot at hosting, but with the same result. It just didn't work.

The men from Don and Ken's company who filmed our show to sell as souvenirs eventually transferred to the Screen Test team as cameramen. Al Gries was one of those guys, and he asked if he could have a shot at hosting.

Upon first impression, I didn't think of Al as a show host. (No offense, Al, if you're reading this.) He was a little quirky, and shorter than the average bear. When the last row of the audience is a long distance away, being bigger helps. But he wanted a chance. Okay, why not.

We worked on his presentation. Al threw himself into it, as I had done in my early years. He wanted to learn and that impressed me. In the end, we developed a persona that worked well for him and he became a very good host. On those days when Pam would call and want me to take off part of the day, I called Al to come in and cover for me.

Back then the studio gave a food allowance at the Flower Drum Song Café to the stuntmen and Screen Test guys. Flower Drum Song Café was a fast-food facility located next to the Woody Woodpecker Theater.

The reason for the free food was to encourage the stuntmen and Screen Test guys to go into the Entertainment Center and be available to talk with guests and take photos rather than sit in the break room between shows. Per our contract, we weren't obligated to do anything other than the show. Truth is, we would have gone out and visited with the guests even without the free food, but it was a nice perk.

Performers were paid a per-show rate, with a minimum of four shows per day. However, in peak seasons (summer, Christmas, Thanksgiving, Easter, Spring Break), we would do as many as fourteen per day.

The stunt team operated differently from Screen Test during those high-attendance days. When multiple stunt shows were scheduled, Lance's team did the first four, then a second team headed by Tom Morga or John Casino did the next four, a third team did the next four, and a fourth team would do the last four, if necessary. (The stunt show could do more shows in a day because their show lasted only twelve minutes.)

But at Screen Test one team did all the shows, whether it was four or fourteen. It was our choice to do them all with one team. And remember, unlike the twelve-minute stunt show, our show lasted thirty-five to forty minutes each. So it was not physically possible to fit more shows into the day.

As the crew was putting away equipment and getting guests out of costumes, I began casting for the next show. It was one after another after another, all day long, on summer days fitting fourteen shows into an eleven-hour day. By the time I got home at night, sometimes as late as 10:00, I was like a zombie. But come show time the next day I was anxious to get the microphone in my hand and back in front of the audience. Did I say how much I loved my job?

One thing *Formica* did *not* love was watching Al eat a burger at Flower Drum Song. There was something about the way he ate it. He went out of his way to make sure the juice ran over his fingers and dripped, more like cascaded, from the burger with every bite. The tomato, lettuce, and meat always hung out the bottom of the bun. It grossed out Formica, and of course Al exaggerated everything just to annoy him.

So, with hundreds of guests sitting around us on the patio at Flower Drum Song, Formica would unfold a paper napkin and hang one end over the top edges of his sunglasses, letting the rest of it hang in front of his face, creating a barrier that blocked his view of Al consuming the burger. It looked odd—Al eating a burger and Formica with a white napkin hanging in front of his face.

One spring day we were sitting around a table on the patio outside the Flower Drum Song. Bees were always an annoyance during the spring and several were buzzing around. Formica was sitting to my right and as a bee buzzed in front of my face I reached up and swatted it in Formica's direction. It caught him at just the right angle and went straight inside his polo shirt. Perfect shot, not that I was aiming. He jumped to his feet and ripped off his shirt in front of the massive crowd filling the patio. The bee escaped and so did Formica without getting stung. Fortunately, he always wore a T-shirt.

The next day we were back on the patio. Again more bees. Formica was sitting to my left. A bee buzzed by and this time I swatted it with my right hand and BAM, it hit Formica and down his shirt, again. He jumped to his feet and the shirt came flying off. True story.

I was in the market for a new car, so one day between shows I wanted to take a quick trip to a car lot several miles away from the studio. Formica wanted to come, and I think Joe came also. (In the slow season we usually had about an hour-and-a-half break between shows.) We piled into Formica's car and took off. I ended up spending more time car shopping than intended, and with show time approaching, we piled back into Formica's car and headed to the studio.

We were flying down the freeway, 90 miles per hour, with only five minutes before I had to begin casting for the show. We were watching the clock. It was gonna be close. Formica commented, "If we get pulled over, we're not gonna get a ticket. We're going to jail." We turned off Lankershim onto the studio property and flew up the hill, whipped into the passenger drop off turn-around, and I jumped from the car and raced for the theater.

Fortunately, Don had taken the initiative and started casting. He saw me coming up the side aisle of the theater and, rather than wait a couple of minutes so I could catch my breath, he introduced me and handed off the microphone. "Thanks," ... pant ... pant ... deep breath ... "Don." I continued panting and gasping for air for the next couple of minutes, but we started on time and finished on time, and the audience was none the wiser.

Formica was, at that time, a reserve police officer for the Burbank PD. He would often regale us with "war" stories. Once he bought a pig mask and would put it on when patrolling with other officers. He told of slipping it on one time as he and his partner pulled up to a red light. A little boy in the car next to them looked over and saw him, then turned to his mom and yelled for her to look. Formica quickly jerked off the mask just before the mom glanced over. He sat staring straight ahead, then looked at the mom and little boy and nodded, official like. The little boy tried his best to convince his mom that the policeman was wearing a pig mask. Formica just smiled.

Universal led the field of movie-monster classics for decades. Films like *Frankenstein*, *Dracula*, *The Wolf Man*, *The Mummy*, and *The Creature from the Black Lagoon* became part of our culture. During the late 70s Universal's tour division thought it would be a good idea to introduce a more user-friendly monster to our guests. How about if Dr. and Mrs. Frankenstein had a kid? (I'm sure the avid movie-monster fan knows that Frankenstein was the name of the doctor who created the Monster.)

Management decided to commission a new character and costume. The birth date for our newest addition was planned and the media invited.

The studio asked me to host the event. I coordinated with Shirley the PR lady. Unfortunately, I can't remember her last name, but she was a master at her trade, and instrumental in the success of Famous Amos Cookies when the company was first getting started.

And so late one morning, with the Woody Woodpecker Theater packed with the press, we began the process of creating the newest member of Universal's cadre of creatures. To ensure an air of mystery we kept the mini-monster concealed under a sheet until the appropriate moment. Then Dr. Frankenstein, dressed in his white lab coat, with his hair frizzed to a light-socket frenzy, threw the switch and the electric current began dancing up and down between the posts.

Suddenly Baby Frankenstein jolted to life! "It's alive! It's alive!" Baby Frankenstein, a cute little character, was about half the size of Daddy. Universal's newest monster had arrived, with lots of good PR from the press. They loved him.

Management decided it would be a good idea if we took Universal Studios on the road—introduce the world to the tour via a traveling road show. So, in the winter of 1978 we began making plans. Our primary venues would be shopping malls and an occasional conference or trade show.

The studio contracted with an outside company to build a three-dimensional set that resembled the exterior of a saloon, complete with swinging doors. The set had to fit in two cases (the size of coffins), and a second requirement was that it had to be easily assembled and taken down.

If YouTube had been around during our first attempt at putting the set together, it would have gone viral. It was comical, to say the least. The first attempt was in the manufacturer's parking lot. We laid out all the pieces then stood back to take a look. It was overwhelming! A bazillion pieces. It took over two hours, and that was with the help of the guys who designed it. But we practiced and practiced. We labeled each piece so we could tell what piece went with another piece, and by the time we left for our first show, we had the time down to about ten minutes.

The road show consisted of three acts, each one about eight minutes in length. The first act was an animal show with Brian Renfro, and featured Fred the Cockatoo from *Baretta*, and Benji the dog.

The second act was a make-up demonstration. Our make-up artist, wearing vampire's teeth, burst from behind the curtain, glided across the stage, and skulked his way through the audience to find just the right lady to transform into the Bride of Frankenstein, complete with costume.

The third act was The Wild West Stunt Show. Tom Morga, Wayne Bauer, and Ray Woodfork re-created a variation of the show from the studio, including fist fights, bullwhips, breakaway bottles, and gun fights. For a show confined to a twenty-by-twenty stage, it was very exciting.

Rounding out the troupe was … me—host and show manager. Before we left for our first show I was encouraged by management to write an introduction that was, honestly, too wordy and flowery. I talked about Hollywood being the dream capital of the world, and anything was possible in the world of movies, etc., etc. To be fair, I tried it. But after the first show on the first day I found that not only was the audience falling asleep, but so was I. So I scratched almost all of it. A thirty second intro, then get Brian, Fred the Cockatoo, and Benji on stage.

We discovered an interesting phenomenon about crowds. They can sometimes be very aggressive over things of insignificant value. Once when on the road, Chicago, I think, we had hundreds of worthless plastic necklaces to give away. Rather than pass them out one by one, we tossed handfuls to the crowd. If observing from a distance, one might think we were giving away hundred-dollar bills. Adults were climbing over each other, sometimes over children. Fingers, hands, and toes were being crushed to get a worthless piece of costume jewelry. We ended up tossing the giveaways in the trash. Those who have been in New Orleans Square at Disneyland may have witnessed the same thing when they toss cheap costume jewelry to the crowds.

Although the studio always booked us coach fare when flying, we usually ended up in first class. After take-off

Brian would reach beneath his seat and take Fred the Cockatoo from the cage and begin doing tricks with him. Before long the flight attendants and those sitting close by, and sometimes even the pilot or co-pilot, would gather around "oohing" and "awing." When that happened, we knew we were headed to first class.

We toured many cities across the country and almost always played to a full house. Mall advertisements read "Universal Studios Coming to […] Mall." Crowds filled every square inch, sometimes thousands of people, and if the mall was two story, the second level was packed as well.

Usually we were booked for a few days then returned home for a few weeks. It was common for us to do three days in Aurora, Illinois, five days in Atlanta, three days in Tampa, a week through northern California, or the Midwest, etc. But in February 1979, we were booked for a month long tour across Canada. And in February, Canada is cold—*really* cold.

Our first stop was Toronto where we spent a few days. A beautiful city. Then we moved on to Winnipeg. What can I say about Winnipeg? Well, actually a lot. But suffice it to say, Winnipeg redefines the word *cold*. Forty-two below! It was the only city I've ever been in that had weather alerts continually running across the bottom of the TV screen. "When outdoors, exposed skin will freeze in sixty seconds." In Winnipeg cars come equipped with extension cords so you can plug it in to keep the oil pan from freezing. And yes, people actually live there, by choice!

I assume the city was beautiful, but who could tell. I will say, they make ice sculptures there in February that give new meaning to the words "art" and "beauty." We aren't talking about small ice sculptures like you see adorning cruise ship dining tables, either.

Winnipeg allows their ice artists to build masterpieces in the median of public streets, and the sculptures fill the median—one was a full-size locomotive, another was a castle that defied the imagination. The detail of each sculpture was unbelievable.

While in Winnipeg, the mall's PR manager and his family invited us to their farm for the day. We had a great time riding their three snowmobiles. Of course when you're with three stuntmen, plus Brain Renfro, who later moved back to Canada and became a stuntman there, it wasn't long before we were doing stunts off the snowmobiles. And sorry to say, by the time we left their house that afternoon, only one Skidoo, as they call it, was still in working condition. Apologies to the family who was so kind to us. After Winnipeg we headed to Calgary.

By that time, I had been away from home for almost three weeks, so Pam flew to Calgary to join me for a short visit. Come to think of it, I was the only married person on the road show. At the time she was six months pregnant with our first son, Matthew (yes, he prefers to be called Matt).

We had no shows the day following Pam's arrival, and sitting around the hotel was out of the question for the guys on the crew, so we rented a van and, along with Pam, headed to Banff to go skiing.

There were six of us on the Universal road show team. Five were experienced skiers, one wasn't. Guess which one? I had lived in Florida, Arizona, and southern California. What's snow?

So while Pam found a cozy spot in the chalet and sipped coffee and hot chocolate, the guys rented boots and skies and headed up the ski lift to one of the highest points on the mountain ... without me. I headed to the bunny slope.

Try as I might, I never once made it down the slope without falling. After a couple of hours of trying, the snow began to fall so hard that Pam could no longer see me as I crashed-and-burned my way up *and* down the hill. Eventually the weather won the day and we headed back to the hotel, after having my first and last attempt at snow skiing.

After Calgary and Edmonton, we finished our tour with three days of shows in Minneapolis, then headed home.

A few years later Pam and I decided to form our own road show company. We rented the set from Universal and hired the stuntmen, make-up artist, and animal trainer (not Brian; he had left the studio by that time). We also hired a host and road-show manager because I was doing shows at Screen Test. But the team was made up of guys I knew and trusted, so we were confident they would do a good job.

It was also about this time that we reinstated the Celebrity of the Day program at Screen Test. Audiences usually arrived early, so a few minutes prior to show time I would introduce our guest star. The celebs would spend five or ten minutes talking with the audience. Some would answer questions and others would do a short monologue.

Among those who paid a visit was George Takei, Sulu in the original cast of *Star Trek*. "Ladies and gentlemen, we have a very special guest with us today. An actor familiar to most of you, especially if you're a fan of *Star Trek*...."

I remember getting to that point and suffering the same mental block I had when introducing Ray Berwick. My mind went blank. I knew his name because I had been talking with him before going on stage for the introduction. But I was drawing a total blank. Of course I had to say his name, so I said to the audience, "Let me check back stage and see if he's ready...." I stuck my head in the door and said to the crew, "What's his name?" Mind you, he was standing just inside the doorway, so I could have asked him. But for some reason that seemed inappropriate. Funny how my mind worked in that moment. Go figure.

"George Takei," the crew replied in unison.

Turn back to the audience. "Yes, he's here. Ladies and gentlemen, please welcome our guest star of the day, George Takei."

I wish I could say that Ray Berwick and George Takei were the only two I drew a mental block with, but sadly, no. It happened a few other times until I finally learned to write their name in the palm of my hand. That way I could glance at my palm as I turned and gestured toward them just prior to their entrance.

Other guest celebrities included Jerry Mathers, from *Leave it to Beaver*, and Walter Koenig, who played Chekov in *Star Trek*. Walter was another one of the forgotten names. What happened to simple names like John Brown or Mary Smith? There were many other celebrities who visited, but you get the idea. That's another way of saying I can't remember who they were.

The Tour Division was (and is) located atop the hill at the studio. In the early days there was also another hill on top of that hill. Inside the second hill was an enormous water tank, a house-sized tank. I was told that when the studio later removed the hill and the tank, it was the largest earth-moving project in California history, up to that time. (I'm not one-hundred percent sure of the accuracy of that statement, but that's what I was told.)

This incident happened in the late 70s or early 80s. Ron Bension had been promoted to a managerial position in the operations department. As the story goes, one evening he drove a company car to the top of the water-tower hill and either he got a little too close to the edge, or the brakes gave out, and the car plummeted to the bottom of the tank. Fortunately, Ron didn't go in with it. The next day a crane had to be brought in to remove the car.

In the late 1970s the boss came and told me a new position had opened up on the lower lot and asked if I was interested in becoming ... a casting director. A casting director? I wanted to be *in* the cast, not choosing the cast! I never pictured myself on the other side of the camera.

Me casting others for roles I wanted to play? Well, okay, I wasn't going to say no. I would take the job and then cast myself. It sounded reasonable to me.

I went through the interview process with a few people over the span of a couple of weeks, then waited for the call. And waited. A week or so later the call came, "Hey, Jerry, we really like you. You're the one we want for that position, but we've been told we have to hire a female." A female? As much as I wanted the job, that's a role I couldn't pull off.

THE 1980s

By this time the tour was in the same league as Disneyland, a first-class theme park, in addition to being the world's largest and busiest motion picture and television studio. We were rockin'!

So, like Disneyland, why not have corporate sponsors? What company wouldn't pay to have their name attached to Universal Studios via a store or restaurant or show? Just imagine: The Acme Screen Test Theater.

Susan Stein, Jay's wife at that time, was given the responsibility of looking for corporations to partner with us. She commandeered the Jack Webb bungalow next to the commissary on the lower lot and set up a meeting room. I was asked to help facilitate the meetings.

We used nine slide projectors programmed to work in concert and produce a presentation that gave the appearance of movement, while using only still pictures. It was pretty cool.

Things were going well. Meetings were taking place and companies were interested. One day there was a corporate sponsorship presentation that my schedule didn't allow me to attend. So I asked Jon Corfino to fill in for me. I brought Jon on board at the Screen Test show as a stage manager. The meeting went well and Jon did a good job. A little too good. Susan and Jon's personalities meshed much better than hers and mine, so I was out as the corporate sponsorship guy. Jon was in. Hmmm.

I often teased Jon about slipping in and stabbing me in the back. But I was okay with it. It wasn't something I really enjoyed doing. I would once again have a brief attachment to corporate sponsorship when the Orlando park was given the green light a few years later.

Compared with today, the footprint of the Entertainment Center was considerably smaller in the 1960s and 1970s. But even back then attendance was growing and the limited space created a problem during peak seasons. At times crowds were so large it was difficult to find a place to put all the guests. So we looked for ways to expand.

One summer we pitched a tent, a circus-sized tent, in a parking lot where the hill with the tank had been removed, about a hundred yards south of the lobby. It was to be a summer carnival setting, a state fair kind of feel. A couple of country/western bands were hired to play in one end of the tent.

But what should we put on the other side? How about a game show? Well, we had never tried that, so why not? Thus was born ... the Show Biz Quiz, a summer show I hosted under the big top in the new area of the park. (Larry also rotated in and shared some of the hosting responsibilities. He worked at Screen Test while I was at Show Biz Quiz, and then we would switch.)

Terry asked me to come up with a game show that would fit the venue. I invited Larry to help and we split our time between the regular duties at the Screen Test show and developing the game show that ended up being a really fun show.

Perhaps I'm a little quirky, but when I write I like to have just the right ambiance, just the right setting. I've tried many, many locations. Some work and some don't, and it usually takes only a minute to find out if I'm in the right place. For me, the right place is usually a local coffee house.

However, when Larry and I were developing the new show, coffee houses were still in the embryo stages and not available on every corner. So we decided to be *creative* at the Sheraton Universal.

Every morning for a couple of weeks, Larry and I would go the coffee shop located one level down from the hotel's main lobby and work on the new show. The restaurant wasn't usually crowded and the staff would give us a corner where we could spread out and get the creative juices flowing. It was great fun.

Most mornings while we were brainstorming and writing, it was common to see Telly Savalas come to the coffee shop for breakfast. His show, *Kojak*, was running at the top of the Nielsen's, and both he and his mom lived at the hotel. If your budget allows, why not live in the penthouse atop the Sheraton. It's even better if the studio will pay for it.

The studio assigned us a budget, smaller than the penthouse budget, and said, "Go find wardrobe for the new show; find a look that fits the venue." Well, in between our three shows a day there were two country music bands entertaining the masses just across the way, and the show was under the big-top, a county-fair atmosphere. So I went to a store in Glendale and bought the most country/western clothes I could find. One shirt was long-sleeved, blue, with white fringe across the chest and back. A second shirt had long, billowy sleeves, and was a maroon color with slits down the sleeve from shoulder to wrist. Black mesh was sewn into the slits. We looked really cool. The first shirt was definitely country/western. In retrospect, the second shirt maybe not so much. But it was still cool looking, and we "fit" the venue. (My son still has one of the shirts, which he wears only to costume parties.)

Game shows always give away prizes. What should our show give as a grand prize? You're probably thinking that the largest, busiest studio in the world would give a car, or a trip to Cancun, maybe Maui. Right? Almost. If you won the Show Biz Quiz, your grand prize was dinner for two at Womphoppers restaurant, an eatery owned by Universal and located a couple of hundred feet from the show.

A stage was constructed for us inside the tent on the opposite side away from the country/western performers. Above the stage were four enormous screens, perhaps ten feet diagonally, with chase lights around each. With our sound track playing in the background, plus the lights chasing around the screens, the show had a really glitzy look.

At the beginning of each show I would go into the audience and select contestants by asking trivia questions. The goal was *not* to stump them with tough questions, but to find eight people who had an engaging personality and who wouldn't put the audience to sleep. The selection process was fun because the audience got involved yelling out answers, trying to help. But it didn't take a movie expert to come up with the right answer to such stumpes as, "What color was the horse in the movie *The Black Stallion*?"

Believe it or not there were occasional guests who couldn't figure it out, so I would help. "The horse was either pink or black." And yes, some guessed pink, so I helped again, "No the other color."

"Black?"

"You're so smart! And you're in the show!" They would bound onto the stage and take a position behind one of two podiums. One podium was identified as the Movie Moguls and the other Television Tycoons. So we had four contestants on each team, similar to a set on *Family Feud*.

We opened with a musical fanfare, accompanied by chase lights and a montage of movies and television shows, plus images of actors and actresses flashing across the giant screens.

I asked the first person at the podium (who served as team captain) the first question (again like *Family Feud*). The team could discuss possible answers among themselves to come up with the correct one, but the captain was the only one who could give the final answer to each question.

"Which of the following actors has performed in the most movies: John Wayne, Jack Lemmon, Christopher Lee, or Jack Wolfman?" (I know, a poor attempt at humor, but that *was* one of the questions.) On occasion captains would guess the least obvious answer, in spite of what their team members might want them to say. There were times when it was evident the team was frustrated with their captain. But we had to stick with the rules—the team captain had to give the final answer.

As I said each actor's name in the multiple-choice question, his or her picture would appear on one of the giant screens behind us, along with the sound effects to give it that special zip. Terry did a great job of designing the stage and effects.

If the correct answer was given by the team captain, lights around that actor's picture would flash and winning music played. If the wrong answer was given, a "honk" would sound. (By the way, although most people guessed John Wayne, Christopher Lee was the correct answer.)

The four contestants functioned as a team until one of the two teams was eliminated. Then the four members of the winning team competed against each other until one person was declared the winner. Then, to win the grand prize, the final contestant had to answer one last question.

For example, "What was the identification number on the Starship *Enterprise*?"

"Hmmm." Tick, tick, tick. The clock counted down. Yes, the time allotted for an answer was limited.

Finally ... "NCC 1701?"

"You are ... absolutely right! You win! Dinner for two at ..." Need I remind you what the prize was? I still get embarrassed when I think of it.

Part of my criticism of the grand prize is in jest. Yes, it didn't have the *wow* factor, but it was logical. If you think about it from a business perspective, we couldn't give away a car or trip to Maui every show. We did three shows a day, seven days a week. That would require a fleet of cars or a hotel in Maui devoted to only us. *Family Feud* doesn't even do that, and they have a much bigger budget than we did. Besides, their show is viewed by millions each night. We played to a few hundred at a time. ROI.

A few years later when I did Q&As with the audience during the Star Trek show, I knew all the Trekkies would know that answer to the identification code on the Starship *Enterprise*, so I asked, "What does the NCC stand for?" No one ever knew that. I'm sure there are Trekkies reading this and jumping up and down, saying "I know the answer! I know the answer! It's...."

Sorry, I'm not saying. If you see me in person, I'll tell you.

(Perhaps I'm being too optimistic is assuming someone other than my family might be reading this book. Now that I think of it, maybe I shouldn't assume my family will read it either.)

Larry and I came up with two sets of questions, thinking we would use one set for the first show and the second set for the second show, then repeat the questions from the first show for the third show of the day. We reasoned that no one would hang around for all three shows. If we repeated the questions from the first show again in the third, we should be safe. Wrong!

It was awkward. One couple stayed and ended up being two of those captains who would not listen to the rest of the team. And the odd part was, even after hearing the questions earlier in the day, they still gave the wrong answers.

The Show Biz Quiz was intended as a summer addition. And so come September we folded our tent, literally, and the show faded into the sunset. Larry and I went back to full-time hosting at the Screen Test Theater. (During our Show Biz Quiz summer, Joe and Al helped cover some of the hosting duties there.)

Attendance in the theme park business usually peaks during summer, Christmas and Easter/spring break. In the early 1980s the amphitheater was still an open-air venue and we needed another "summer show" to spread the crowds around the park. On peak days we were exceeding thirty-thousand guests a day.

That's Incredible and *Those Amazing Animals* were two popular television shows at the time, and the studio thought it would be entertaining if we created a live stage version of those shows for the Universal amphitheater.

The show *That's Incredible* starred John Davidson, Kathy Lee Crosby, and Fran Tarkenton (the same Fran Tarkenton who quarterbacked the Minnesota Vikings). The other TV show we drew from was *Those Amazing Animals*, which starred Priscilla Presley (Elvis' former wife), Jim Stafford, and Burgess Meredith. (That's a great trivia question because most people remember Burgess Meredith as an accomplished actor, yet few people know that he hosted a show of that nature.)

How were the acts selected from *That's Incredible* and *Those Amazing Animals*, and meshed together for a theater that seated over five-thousand guests? I have no idea.

The shows were very different. The reasoning behind the selection was a mystery, and still remains so today. The producers of the TV show selected the acts for us. I would have chosen differently.

I was asked to host the show. I knew it would be challenging because two of the three acts included a single person on stage in a very big theater. The first row of the audience was quite a distance from the stage, and the last row required a rest stop to get there. So I needed to engage the audience to help them feel involved.

The only way to do that was through me. (No, it wasn't an "ego" thing.) They couldn't be on stage, but I was the constant throughout the show. They could experience it through me. It's the host's responsibility to keep the audience involved. By helping them identify with me, I took their place and they engaged. So I came up with introductions and segues, and then worked out dialogue with two of the three acts that allowed the audience to be involved.

The first act was a "breathairian." You're probably asking, "What's a breathairian"? That was my question when first meeting him. According to the breathairian, it's someone who doesn't eat food. No food! He explained that he received his nutrition, his food, from the air. Oh, really?

Now there's an endless number of jokes you could do with that in the early 1980's, especially living in Los Angeles. But that was his claim—no food. Five thousand people sat listening to a very, very thin man talk about eating the air.

He claimed to be very strong as a result of his unique diet and lifted weights on stage to prove his point. However, between shows backstage, out of view of the public, the breathairian snacked … yes, real food, albeit fruit. So much for eating the air. (I'm can only imagine what he ate at home.)

Usher the breathairian off stage (quickly) and on with our second act. A team of four martial artists offered a well-rounded display of jumps and kicks, leaps and rolls. Their act included a mind-over-matter demonstration when one of the guys stuck a needle (the size of a knitting needle) through his forearm without drawing blood ... usually. The needle-through-the-arm routine became even more entertaining when mind-over-matter failed and blood started flowing from the guy's arm. And that happened more than once. So I would make a few lighthearted comments and try to distract the audience. Was it more exciting than the breathairian? What wouldn't be? But if you're sitting a hundred-and-fifty feet away, who could really appreciate a needle through the arm. Most of the audience couldn't even seen the needle.

The third act—I remember it much more vividly than the others —was the Amazing Joe Acton. Joe's act held my attention, one-hundred percent. Why? Because it involved a diamondback rattlesnake. A real one! And I was on stage with it, just a few feet away. Snakes. "Why'd it have to be snakes?"

Joe and I chatted for a couple of minutes and then he would make the claim that he had the fastest hands in the world.

"Sugar Ray Leonard makes the same claim," I reminded him. (Sugar Ray was at the height of his boxing career at that time.)

"Let me prove it," he would say and then tip the burlap sack he was holding upside down. A full-sized, adult diamondback rattlesnake plopped out onto a small platform. The platform was about chest high and had plexiglass on three sides so the audience could watch.

At that point yours truly backed away ... quickly ... although I remained close enough for the audience to experience fear through me.

Joe let the snake writhe for a few seconds, then began slapping the table next to the snake. Finally, after being sufficiently irritated, the snake would do what snakes do when cornered—strike. Joe's trick was to catch the snake just before it struck his face. I watched it, up close and personal. There was nothing fake about Joe's act. Just to keep it interesting, he would get a new snake every couple of days. And for some reason the new snake always looked bigger than the previous one.

On the final show of the final day we went through our usual routine. Joe made his claim about having the fastest hands in the world, which of course I challenged. "Let me prove it!" he replied, then tipped over the burlap sack and out plopped *two* rattlesnakes. Surprised? You bet. I remember the snakes hissing as they slithered away from each other. But with no place to go, they coiled against the plexiglass in opposite corners of the three-foot-wide platform. As I said, Joe's two-snake-plan for the last show came as a complete surprise to me. Up to that point it had been only one snake per show.

He began slapping the table, first one side then the other. Finally, both snakes had enough and lunged at him within a split-second of each other. Snatch, snatch. Faster than the blink of an eye, Joe grabbed both snakes just inches from his face. He told me after the show that was the first time he tried the two-snake grab. It was information I was glad to know *after* the fact.

Joe's claim to having the fastest hands in the world had my vote. I was hoping the audience experienced the danger and fear, and felt a part of the show, through me.

That's Incredible and Those Amazing Animals were different experiences, maybe even fun, but not the right shows for a venue like the amphitheater. The theater was too large for such a small show. (Small as in having a visual impact on the audience from such a distance.)

Another reason the shows fell short, in my opinion, was … a breathairian. Really? Even if the act had been real, who believed it, or cared?

Summer ended and I was back at Screen Test, but it wasn't long before the show needed a facelift, a complete new look. The Airport '77 show had been good, but it was from 1977. Kinda dated.

We began brainstorming ideas for a new Screen Test show. What would fit our venue, entertain our guests, and at the same time give Jay something new to advertise? How about an earthquake? Let's do a show based on the movie *Earthquake*, that starred my old buddy Charlton Heston. (If only.)

We kicked around the idea. It sounded good. With 1980s technology we could come up with a great show. Enclosing the theater and making it into an indoor venue would make it even better.

As we explored the concept we wanted our guests to have the experience of a real earthquake. Exterior walls of the theater would be stone, wood, or stucco, but the interior walls would be screens as big as the walls themselves. We would project onto the screens what looked like normal interior walls, perhaps drapes, sconces, and decorative artwork.

At some point in the show the floor would begin to shake, first gently, then increasingly more violent. Ceiling light fixtures would sway as the interior walls of the theater appeared to crumble. As the interior walls projected on the screens began to topple we would project on the giant wall what appeared to be the area outside the theater and people scrambling for their lives. All the while the floor of the theater would continue to shake.

Hit the brakes! Maybe that's a little too realistic. Lew Wasserman agreed. After hearing the concept, he put a kibosh on the whole idea. He felt it would be too scary for our guests since we weren't that far removed from the 1971 Sylmar earthquake, centered just a few miles from the studio. He was probably right. A little too realistic. But it would have been a great show.

Wasserman always considered the Screen Test show his favorite. He said our show provided what the guests really came for, a chance to be a star. I enjoyed reminding the other show performers of that as often as I could.

In 2005 Wasserman was the subject of a TV biography called *The Last Mogul*. He *was* the last of the Hollywood moguls. The documentary was an excellent look at his sway and influence over the industry.

Screen Test number six was probably the most "fun'"show we every did. Adam-12 was the easiest, but The Great Chase was the most fun, even though the storyline of the show was kind of lost in the fun of it.

It began with a bank robbery in the Old West. At the beginning of the mini-movie a bag was stolen from the bank, but the contents of the bag contained a surprise that wasn't revealed until the end. The bag becomes the transition piece that took us from one decade to the next, ending with scenes from the movie *The Blues Brothers*.

The scenes were: 1) a bank robbery in the Old West where the bag and its mysterious contents were stolen, 2) the bank robbers were pursued on horse back by the posse, 3) the robbers jumped into a river and lost the bag in the fast-moving water, 4) the bag floated down the river and was picked up by a couple, Wilbur and Maude, from the 1920's era, out for a romantic afternoon row down a turbulent river. When the couple encountered the rapids, Wilbur tossed the bag into the air, 5) where it was caught by an escaped prisoner flying overhead in a bi-wing plane. (Exciting, huh!) The bi-plane ended up flying upside down and the bag fell, 6) into the outstretched arms of John Belushi from *The Blue Brothers*. Each time a new person gained possession of the bag and opened it, a surprised expression was required.

As you can tell, the storyline required a stretch of the imagination.

The sets included the Old West bank, four fake horses mounted on springs, the tank for the river scene (held over from Airport '77), a row boat mounted on a gimbal that spun and tilted, a two-seater bi-wing plane that rotated to fly upside down, and the front portion of the *Blues Brothers'* car in a bakery set.

The show had more cameos of movie stars than could be counted, from Buster Keaton to John Wayne to Dan Aykroyd. It was a movie-star extravaganza.

Oh, and the mystery in the stolen bag—a whipped cream pie. It was removed from the bag in the final scene (a bakery set), and a pie fight broke out.

Now you understand why I said the premise was lost in the fun. And it was fun. Almost everyone from the audience who participated got either soaking wet or hit in the face with a pie. Ladies came on stage with lovely hairdos, but by the end of the show they were matted and plastered to their heads with whipped cream, or completely soaked from jumping into the tank of water. But anything for show biz.

Wilbur and Maude were doused with buckets and buckets of water as the boat spun around, first in one direction, then I would twist the control knob and throw them in the opposite direction. People were jumping from ledges into the river, whipped cream was being smeared into faces, up nostrils, and in ears. It was amazing how cooperative people were. Guests weren't just *willing* to be in the show, they were anxious to do it. The stories I could tell.

Our audience volunteers were respectable, everyday people—bankers, brick layers, judges, school teachers, janitors, lawyers—people from every walk of life. But when on stage with the cameras rolling, look out! We even had a visit from the Queen. Yes, the one from England. She really knows how to take a pie in the face. No, not really. Secret Service frowned on hitting Her Majesty in the face with a pie. Party killer.

When thinking back on the countless shows we did at Stage 70 and Screen Test, it's amazing that we rarely had anyone injured. Guests, untrained in acting or stunts, did some remarkable things, and with only a few minutes' rehearsal.

However, there was one incident when the stage manager dropped the stolen bag to the escaped prisoner in the bi-plane and hit him in the forehead. Foreheads bleed profusely and, although it looked as if we had taken off his head, it was just a minor gash. The man went to the nurse's station for repair, then returned later wanting to do it again. You gotta love show biz.

Being a part of the Screen Test crew was always a blast. Everyone lived with the understanding that we were always fair game when on stage. If there was a way to get one of us to crack up in front of the audience, especially the guy with the microphone, then chances were....

The console which I operated during the show controlled all of the special effects on stage. There were probably twenty buttons, about an inch in diameter, so I could easily get to them while at the same time talking with the audience and giving cues to the guest actors.

One summer day we were in the middle of a show and Al was running camera. As I recall, I made a joke to the audience about him chewing gum on stage, then continued on with the show. When I came back to the console I noticed that Al was no longer chewing gum. Then I spotted it, a large wad of chewed gum laying across the button I had to push for the upcoming effect. Al was trying his best to control his laughter. He knew I had no option but to push that button.

The show was in full swing. I was talking to the audience and at the same time giving direction to our guests as we recorded the next scene. Al was focused on getting that shot.

Yes, I could be considered a germaphobe, but forget the germs, that day I was determined. So while carrying on with the show, I worked very carefully and maneuvered the edges of Al's gum until I got it in a ball.

By that time the scene was over and I call, "Cut!" The crew immediately began readying for the next scene, which meant that Al went to a different part of the stage to move equipment and get the guests ready for our next shot.

I explained the next scene to the audience and had a brief conversation with the guest actors. Al finished his setup and returned to his camera and slipped on his headset—still with that annoying little smile on his face. I carried on as if everything was good. And to me it was.

Then Al looked at the console and saw the chewing gum was missing from the button, but by that time we were already into the next scene. Now his focus was divided—get the shot, look for the gum.

As I talked with the audience, I watched his eyes. He was grabbing quick glances here and there, trying to find the gum. He didn't know where it was, but he knew that wherever it was, it wasn't good.

"And cut!" The scene ended. Al reached up to remove his headset and suddenly realized where the gum was. (Al always wore his hair in kind of a Beatles "do," covering just below his ears.) As he pulled the headset away, long strings of chewing gum strung out between the headset and his ear, his hair matted in the strings of chewing gum. It took all I could do to keep it together. I was dying on the inside, and the audience could tell something was cracking me up. I pretended it was the performance of the guest actors on stage.

Al's only solution was to quickly yank the headset away, carry on, and deal with getting the chewing gum out of his hair after the show. Scissors would be involved.

My desire was still there. I wanted to be a movie star. Formica was attending acting classes in Hollywood and asked me to come with him and check it out. Okay, why not? I'd at least had some prior training, at Estelle Harmon's workshop many years earlier, and later at Valley College and Cal State Northridge.

The Van Mar Academy was owned by Ivan Markota. They were holding classes in his home on my first visit because a fire had destroyed their theater several weeks earlier. The room was crowded with fellow thespians and Ivan proved to be an excellent instructor. It was the best training I could have hoped for. He had an array of students that went on to become household names, including Bryan Cranston, Mariska Hargitay, John Larroquette, and Mary Hart.

After several weeks meeting in his home, he opened a theater on Melrose Avenue and we continued there until I left the school a year or two later.

Ivan died in 2013 at the age of eighty-six. He was a great acting coach.

Back to Universal, Terry was busy, and you didn't have to look far to find his imprint. By now he had built many attractions, and had served as executive vice president and also general manager of the tour. He oversaw the design, development, and rise of the tour during its formative years.

But things change. So in 1982 Terry, being so versatile, was offered the job of general manager of the San Diego Zoo and Wild Animal Park. The zoo was in need of someone to bring order, money-saving ideas, and increased attendance.

It was a sad time when he left. To me, Terry was Universal. Everywhere I looked I saw his influence.

However, several months after Terry landed in San Diego, he called. He was putting in a summer show at the zoo's amphitheater and wanted me to host it. It was a show with Joan Embery, the zoo's good-will ambassador.

A live stage-show at the zoo? Hmmm. He envisioned three shows a day, three days a week—Friday, Saturday and Sunday. Of course I would do it, if for no other reason than Terry asked. But first I needed permission from Universal.

One day, shortly after Terry's offer, I ran into Jay Stein in the park and told him of Terry's request. Jay really liked Terry, and said I had always been a good employee, then gave his permission. So with that affirmation the plan was for me to work at Screen Test twelve to fourteen shows a day, Monday through Wednesday, then travel to San Diego on Thursday and do three shows a day at the zoo, Friday through Sunday. Doing that number of shows a day at the zoo compared to Universal would be a walk in the park....

The idea of doing shows at the aoo was appealing. It was one more thing to add to the résumé. Pam and the kids might even accompany me from time to time. As it turned out they went *every* weekend. I spent the summer doing three shows a day for which Terry paid me well. But come September, I ended up breaking even because, while I was slaving over a hot microphone, Pam and the kids were shopping every day and eating ice cream sundaes at Farrell's. The whole "zoo summer" was wonderful; an experience the family still talks about today.

So what kind of show would work at the zoo? Obviously, a show with animals. The show was already in rehearsal in the zoo's amphitheater, but Terry wanted to add a different element. His background was entertainment. The zoo's approach was more narrative, educational. I just needed to modify what was already there, not create a show from scratch.

I remember driving down to see the show. Terry and I sat and watched a rehearsal. We were the only two in the thousand-seat amphitheater. The stage was about forty-feet across and twenty-five-feet deep, with a couple of exits to backstage. A four-foot-wide moat ran the full width of the stage, separating it from the audience.

The announcer came on stage and greeted the would-be audience, and then introduced Joan. She entered carrying a koala. The announcer stepped back a few feet and knelt down on one knee. From that point on he assumed the role of "helper," bringing out animals as Joan talked about one after another. It was fifteen minutes of a talking head, as I called it.

In addition to being a really nice lady, Joan was the consummate expert on all things animal; an encyclopedia of knowledge on everything that made it off the ark. And could she talk! Her approach was to give the audience as much information as possible in the fifteen-minute show. Information overload!

Terry and I sat and watched the show. Informative but not very entertaining. So about half way through the show I said to Terry, "I'll be right back." I went down to the stage and asked if we could start again from the top. Imagined drum roll. I came on stage and welcomed our vast audience of one (Terry), then introduced Joan. She came out and walked downstage a few feet past me as she had done previously, then began her usual narrative. I immediately took several giant steps forward and positioned myself right next to her. I saw Terry in the audience nod his head and smile with approval. Joan glanced left, saw me, but kept talking. I'm sure she wondered why this guy was standing beside her.

I waited for her to take a breath in her narrative at which point I was going to jump in with a comment or question. But she didn't come up for air. I waited, but she kept talking. Finally I forced an interruption with a question, she responded, then went back to her spiel. Again, I waited for a chance to interject. No such luck. So I jumped in again with a joke, followed by a comment. She laughed and responded, and then I could see it in her eyes, she got it. It was going to be an entertaining talk show, not a lecture.

The only difference between a regular talk show and ours was that our guests had four legs rather then two. But to make it entertaining we needed to bring the audience across the proscenium onto the stage—figuratively, not literally.

That evening I spent time coming up with questions I could ask, because I knew whatever I asked, Joan could answer. I also thought through several scenarios to engage the audience.

The next morning Joan and I met at a restaurant inside the zoo and discussed our approach. The animals used on stage were not show animals, they were animals taken from the wild. So a lot of the content that ended up in the show came as a result of spur-of-the-moment actions or reactions.

One of our guest animals was an elephant. Joan thought it would be fun to have the elephant wrap its trunk around my neck. Cute, but all that ran through my mind was, if this elephant sneezes, my head is coming off. And elephants have been known to be unpredictable. And the skin on their trunk is rough. And....

She also thought it would be fun to see if she could get a zebra to take a handkerchief out of my back pocket. It doesn't sound like a big deal, but zebras are difficult animals to train, so teaching it to take a handkerchief out of my back pocket was an accomplishment. (The zebra didn't know or care where the handkerchief ended and my backside began. I had marks to prove it.)

The show turned out to be great fun, and funny. The audience really seemed to enjoy it.

In addition to the usual array of animals that paraded across the stage, Terry arranged for a "guest animal" star-of-the-day. Perhaps the most famous was the black stallion from the movie *The Black Stallion*.

But the animal that was indelibly imprinted on my mind was a bear, a full-sized grizzly bear. When standing on stage with the bear only ten feet away, "full sized" doesn't really describe him. BIG! And no matter how tame a wild animal is, they remain a wild animal.

How did we accommodate Joan, me, the handler, and the griz on stage at the same time? It wasn't all that complicated, which actually concerned me. I would have appreciated a more sophisticated form of protection.

One single strand of a sixteen-gauge wire was stretched around the perimeter of the stage, but leaving an area on the side, stage left, about three wide, where Joan and I stood. The wire was connected to a battery. The theory was, if the bear charged Joan or me, a person backstage would hit the switch and the current running through this *tiny* little wire would be a deterrent to stop him from killing us.

I had a different theory—an eight-foot-tall bear weighing over six-hundred pounds might not even feel the current running through a wire that was slightly bigger than a human hair. He might look at it as a challenge before snack time.

But then I remembered the advice I'd heard from others. If the bear charged, I didn't have to outrun him, I just had to outrun Joan. Chivalry or self-preservation? Tough choice.

The show had a great run, but summer ended and we said good-bye to Terry, Joan, the stage crew, and the animals, then headed home to Universal.

The Great Chase Show had been running successfully for a few years.

I know it might appear that I spent very little time at the studio, but I really did. Like I said, over thirty-two thousand shows at Stage 70 and Screen Test, and that number doesn't include the extras like the zoo and road shows.

The Screen Test show had three classifications of personnel—the show performers, stage managers, and what we called "briefers." Briefers were those who rehearsed the guests in their role prior to the show starting. They also stood nearby while we were filming to assure that guests hit their cues when I called for them.

After several years our lead stage manager, Adrian, who just happened to be ranked as one of the top ten judo masters in the world, was leaving the show. He had become a key part of our team and we couldn't let him leave without a proper send off. (This incident happened before the first show of the day, so there was no audience and no one in the park.)

The crew decided to take Adrian up onto the ledge and throw him into the tank of water stage right. At least that was my understanding. Several guys grabbed him and headed toward the tank while I went to the console on stage to push the flood-button.

There were two sets of stairs leading to the tank. The first three steps led to the side entrance, then if you continued up past that landing another ten or twelve steps, you reached the top ledge where guests would leap into the "river," or as was our intent that morning, throw someone into the river.

Somewhere between the time I left them to go to the console and their reaching the stairs, they decided to open the side door and put him in, close the door, and then I was to flood the tank. Remember that submarine-style door I mentioned earlier? Well, just about the time they turned the door handle, I pushed the console button, and once it's pushed there ain't *no* stopping it. Six thousand gallons of water was heading their way, and the door was open. Ten men could not close the door, much less the four of them.

The water slammed against the door, knocked them into the handrail, washed them down the stairs, onto the stage, and bounced them around like pinballs. The water poured over the apron of the stage and out into the park. It was like the Colorado River churning up whitewater though the Entertainment Center and toward a drain fifty yards away.

Guess who was walking the park that morning? Ron Bension, the general manager. He carefully maneuvered his way around the flood and to the edge of the stage where I was standing. He looked up at me and with half a smile said, "Some days you just can't get away with anything."

A couple of hours later we received a call from Mike Hoffer, the entertainment manager. "What are you guys doing over there?" We explained and he understood, but had to make the call so he could tell Ron that he took care of it. I don't really think Ron cared, either. It was protocol.

Ron, by the way, began at Universal as a park attendant. (Their job was to keep the park clean.) In his early years he used to hide out at Stage 70 and sleep in the technical director's booth between shows.

But his brother Marc, who was a manager and helped get him the job, threatened Ron to get his act together or he would fire him. Ron did just that. He got it together, and as they say, the rest is history. Ron was eventually promoted to the operations office and when Cliff Walker left, Ron became the manager. Ron was a good manager, different from my style of management, but it fit Jay's style. And it was Jay's style that mattered. He would soon become the general manager.

When Ron moved to operations he also brought with him Felix Mussenden. Felix would later become general manager at Universal Orlando, and eventually president of Universal Studios Escape.

One day three men from the maintenance department were working at the show making repairs. It was between shows, but I happened to be crossing the stage and overheard one of the guys joking with the other two and swearing loudly, using offensive, gross language. Although the curtains were closed, I was concerned that someone might be waiting in the audience for the next show and hear the conversation. Perhaps even kids could be within ear shot. As I said earlier, I was extremely protective of our guests. My fuse was ignited and I came down on him hard in front of the other guys, for using inappropriate language in a family environment.

Afterward, I felt really bad. It wasn't that correcting him was wrong, but doing it the way I did, in front of the others, was wrong. Lenny was an acquired taste, kind of rough around the edges, but the truth was, I liked him. His brother, Tony, also worked in the maintenance department. Completely different personalities. I heard that Lenny passed away a few years ago and I always regretted not apologizing to him for the confrontation.

Another incident (this one I wasn't part of) happened around this same time and was perpetrated by a tour guide who was quitting the studio for another job the following day. On his last tour of the day he thought he would vent and went completely off the tracks, intentionally. It was reported that while giving his tour on the tram he was making rude and offensive comments about Lew Wasserman and other management personnel, swearing, and in general, being an idiot, a jerk! That's the kind of person you'd like to get your hands on for a few minutes just before they kicked him out the front gate.

I was told that management heads rolled over the incident, because when they heard it was happening he was allowed to finish the tour rather than send someone to replace him. (I wasn't at the studio that day, so to be honest I'm not sure if he was removed from the tram or allowed to finish the tour.)

In 1984, Pam and I found out we were going to have another kid. Surprise, surprise! Jonathan Adam would be born in May of the following year. (He prefers to be called Jonathan. Finally.) Now we had two boys and two girls. The perfect number. Why the perfect number? It's simple logic—one kid, spoiled; two kids, bickering; three kids, it's two against one; four kids, the perfect balance. How do I know? It's simple, we had four and none were refundable. Hence four *had* to be the perfect number. (More *jerryosophy*.)

As the years passed, my kids grew up around the park, visiting frequently, and to this day theme parks are an integral part of their lives. Suzi and Kimi, not as much as the boys, but they still love it. Suzi worked at the park on two different occasions. Kimi lives in Phoenix and is very involved in community theater. Matthew has drifted more toward the production side of entertainment, film making, plus teaching film and writing at the Master's University in southern California. For our youngest son, Jonathan, theme parks are wholly engrained in his DNA. To say he's passionate would be to understate the severity—he visits Universal at least a couple of hundred times a year, and almost the same with Disney. Plus, he's been to every Disney and Universal Park in the world, except Paris.

About the same time as Jonathan came along, Universal was opening another special effect—King Kong. I was asked to host the press event to be held on the lower lot. On event day I donned the safari costume of the character Mr. Denham, and made ready. The press gathered, along with studio execs and celebs. As the morning hours ebbed the excitement grew. Finally, show time, and....

Action! Military jeeps raced in from all sides of the area, actors in military uniforms were preparing for the incoming "creature." Tension filled the air. Army personnel rushed in and lined the area in front of me, and just as I finished my spiel, the cue was given.

Suddenly, out of nowhere, a helicopter streaked across the sky just above the press. Hanging precariously beneath the chopper was a huge container, thirty-five feet in length, being tossed about by the downdraft. After a dramatic approach, the helicopter circled overhead kicking up dust hundreds of feet in every direction, then set the container down, hitting the mark precisely. Cameras flashed and people jockeyed for the best position.

Then a guttural growl echoed from inside the container, followed by crashing sounds as a huge hairy fist burst through the side of the oversized crate. King Kong had arrived, and he was ticked!

After the fist of the thirty-foot-tall gorilla crashed through the container the show was over. A short presentation, yes. But the press ate it up and followed that by generating great publicity for our newest attraction.

In the mid-1980s I received a call one day from the head of HR asking me to come to his office. Yikes! What's up with that? Well, come to find out that, much to my surprise, I was offered the job of entertainment manager, a position held by Mike Hoffer, a friend dating back to our tour-guide days. I was told that Mike was leaving and they wanted me to fill in on an interim basis while they looked for his replacement. Again, one of those "hmmm" moments.

I loved doing shows, so entertainment manager would mean an office position and no more performing. I asked if I could have a few hours to think it over, drove to a coffee shop in Toluca Lake and thought it over, then I found a phone booth and called Pam.

She knew how much I loved doing shows, and understood the great relationship we guys had at Screen Test, but as always, she was fully supportive of whatever I decided. "Okay, I'll do it."

I drove back to the head of HR's office and told him I would take the job. So, effective the next day, I became only the second entertainment manager Universal ever had, up to that point. The position eventually morphed into the title of director of entertainment, but that title came with more money, so in the beginning it was "manager." (A month later I would officially accept the position in a permanent capacity.)

My new responsibilities included oversight of all the shows, the Knight Rider interactive car, show control personnel, He-Man (Master of the Universe), Barbie and the Rockers, after-hours concerts at the Screen Test Theater, Halloween Horror Nights, plus the strolling characters, e.g., Frankenstein, Dracula, Charlie Chaplin, Groucho Marx, Woody Woodpecker, and much more.

The entertainment office was located in back of the Woody Woodpecker Theater. It was a small space that previously served as dressing rooms for the marionette show performers. (The show had been cancelled a few years prior.)

To say the office was small was an understatement. And to describe it as cluttered, even more so. My predecessor, Mike, was great with people and a good friend, but not very organized. So my first goal was to get a handle on what was in the office, buried under the piles of paperwork and other stuff scattered and piled around the tiny space. I was never a workaholic like Terry, but I knew it was going to take a few late nights at the office to get things organized.

The location and condition of an office says a lot about what corporate thinks about a department. The entertainment department's location and condition said to everyone, "It's a department, but not a very important one." To most people it was thought of as a stepchild of the operations department. Even the operations department thought of it as a stepchild to them. The location and condition of the windowless office, as well as the relationship to Operations, were issues I would have to address, but later. First things first. Let's get the department running smoothly and efficiently.

Ron Bension had already hired Myles McNamara to replace Rick Trenholme as Mike's assistant. So he would continue as my assistant. Myles was an excellent manager and remains a friend even today. We run into each other on a fairly regular basis at the local coffee house.

My second goal was to hire a secretary. Up to that time, Mike and Myles handled all phone calls and visitors themselves. I reasoned that a hundred-million-dollar department should have a secretary, someone to answer the phone and assist with administrative duties.

After getting Myles' input, we brought in one of the ladies who worked as a show control supervisor—Teresa. As it turned out, Teresa was a no-nonsense young lady who was not always user-friendly. She was known to shoot first and ask questions later. Flak jackets were available to those braving our front door. It was easier to field dress a live porcupine than get past her.

There were five shows in the entertainment center: the stunt show, the animal show, the Screen Test show, the A-Team show, and now … the Adventures of Conan.

Prior to the arrival of the Adventures of Conan, the theater had been home to several other shows, including the stunt show, Stage 70, the Land of a Thousand Faces, and Castle Dracula. But visually and technically, the Adventures of Conan show was the most spectacular. Although the show never lived up to the ratings Jay Stein hoped for, the team from Landmark Entertainment produced what was probably the most visually engaging show ever at the tour.

The theater was completely enclosed except for two entrances, one on each side of the stage. (Unfortunately the entrance locations were the only negative to the show. But that wasn't the fault of Landmark. They inherited the theater design.)

A rain curtain added another layer of mystery. A constant flow of water, falling like a curtain from overhead pipes, allowed the guests to see a vague semblance of what awaited when the show began. I consider the rain curtain to be one of the most dramatic effects in any show. It set the tone for something special that awaited the audience.

Show time. The rain curtain "parted" to reveal a stage decorated as a ruined temple filled with treasure. The twenty-minute show included sword fights, lasers, explosions, a high fall and ... wait for it—a fourteen-foot-tall fire-breathing dragon that rose from a pit center stage writhing and roaring, towering over Conan, while shooting real fire from its mouth.

Gary Goddard and his team did a great job of designing and producing a show that could only be described as spectacular.

I quickly discovered the most important thing necessary to keep the actors happy and content at the Conan show—mirrors, lots of mirrors. All of the performers, except one, were dyed-in-the-wool, chiseled-physique, I-count-my-carbs body builders. There was more body oil and testosterone backstage at the Conan show than at any other single location on the planet.

One day I was in Victoria Station restaurant, adjacent to the tour entrance, having lunch. Richie, one of the actors who played the Conan character, came in, in costume—which was just a loin cloth. I watched as he went from table to table talking with customers and sampling food from everyone's plate. As he chatted with the guests, he would pick things off their plate and eat it! Being a germaphobe, I found that wrong on so many levels. But of course most of the customers had just seen him at the show, so they were more than anxious to visit with Conan. Richie had the kind of personality that allowed him to get away with that, so I let it pass. Victoria Station actually liked it. He brought in the customers and provided entertainment, of a sort.

Managing the entertainment department required wearing several hats. I recall spending time with one of the show warriors to help him understand how to take a hit during a fight sequence. He was a body-builder, not an actor, trying to learn stage fighting. His dilemma seemed to be a simple fix. He wasn't making the fight believable. A right-handed punch was thrown, but for some reason Kevin kept snapping his head in the same direction as the punch was coming from. It didn't matter how many times I tried to help him understand that his head should snap in the direction away from the fist. "You see, Kevin, if someone punches you from the right, your head would snap to the left." He just couldn't grasp the concept. Eventually, I learned to live with it, because he had. And it was far enough from the audience that it didn't impact the show.

The stunt show, animal show and screen test shows continued as usual and, aside from an occasional personnel issue, ran smoothly. Then there was the the A-Team Live-Action Stunt Show.

"Ah, yes, the A-Team show," he says with a sigh. It was a show with great potential on paper, but always fell short. Not that it was a bad show; it had many individual entertaining elements. But when wrapped up and presented as a package, it came up lacking. It disappointed in two ways: it lacked enough "show" to fill the A-Team arena, and it failed in the staging.

Based on the hit television show, the live stage version took place in an outdoor arena, perhaps a hundred-fifty feet across, and seated three-thousand people. The show included the Hannibal and B.A. Baracus characters, plus world-class moto-cross stunt cyclists.

In addition to multiple motorcycle ramp-jumps, twenty-five to thirty feet across the arena, the show also included the A-Team van jumping a broken bridge, a dune buggy flipping side-over-side and coming to rest upside down in a small lake, and a zip line stretched between two buildings. Like I said, many individual elements that were very exciting.

One day I received a call from the A-Team show. "Come quickly, there's had been an accident." I hustled over and found the person playing the Hannibal character had fallen from the zip line twenty feet down, landing on his back. The emergency team was called and he was rushed to St. Joseph's Hospital in serious condition.

I hopped in the car and followed the ambulance. Needless to say, he was severely injured. His breathing was labored because of broken ribs and damaged internal organs. It was obvious he wasn't going home anytime soon. His wife arrived and was understandably distraught.

Rather than have her drive back and forth from home to the hospital each day, we arranged for her to stay at the Hilton, located next to the Sheraton Universal. His recovery was slow and his health prevented him from coming back to the show.

I got a call one morning that Jay was coming to see the A-Team show. I walked over there to be available should he have questions or comments. He watched the show with Ron Bension then got up and left. No comments, no questions.

About an hour later I received a call. "Come to Jay's office." Well, that can't be good. I drove down the hill to the black tower. Jay was located on the fourteenth floor, so up the elevator I went. As I entered, there was Jay, Ron, and Bernie Fisher, Jay's right hand man.

It's fair to say that Jay was a little upset about the A-Team show he watched earlier. After several minutes of ranting about the show he said (this part of the conversation is imprinted in my mind), "I want you to fire everyone of those ******* A-Team performers."

I took a few seconds to let the air settle, and then told him, "Okay, Jay, I'll go back and fire them all, but I want you to know I'll be firing some of the best bikers in the world. We aren't going to find guys who can do it better."

"They didn't look like the best to me!" he fired back. "I could jump a motorcycle farther than they did."

"Jay," I replied, "it was the first show of the day. Sometimes the first show is tough. That's not an excuse. It should be a good show every time, because our guests pay for that. But they just had a bad show. It happens sometimes. Every show isn't a hundred percent."

There were several seconds of silence, then I saw a change in Jay, one I had never seen before. His demeanor shifted. I remember him shaking his head, "I don't want to fire them. I'm just so frustrated with that show."

That I understood. It was that kind of show.

After the dust cleared I didn't fire them, but did relay that the boss was not pleased and they needed to step up their game, every time, even the first show of the day.

They were surprised to hear their performance was lacking, because they knew Jay was in the audience and thought they had done a good show. But sometimes it happens. Energy can be low and you don't realize it. Or you can lose focus and performance suffers. However, when you're jumping motorcycles twenty feet up in the air and landing thirty feet away, it's always good to stay focused.

Fortunately, aside from the zip-line incident, we never had a significant injury at A-Team. But the zip-line injury was more than enough.

I do recall a time when some of the performers came to me with concerns about one of their peers. They felt he was unsafe to work with. What do you do when those kinds of issues are brought up? If you ignore them and someone gets hurt, who's to blame? The person who ignored the warnings.

It was obvious that I couldn't put the other performers in the position of working with him if they felt unsafe. So I did some quick investigating, then contacted Human Resources to be sure I followed protocol.

I then called in another stuntman to cover the last A-Team show of the evening. The next call was to the performer in question and asked him to come to my office. I explained the situation, without mentioning names, after which he told his side of the story. I was confident he wasn't intentionally acting in an unsafe manner, but I couldn't put the other performers at risk, especially since they brought the objections to me. This all happened with a two- or three-hour window.

He was a part-time substitute performer, so I didn't know him that well, and I wasn't sure how he would react to the news of being fired. The thought crossed my mind that I might have a fight on my hands. But to his credit, after realizing the inevitable, he removed his A-Team wrist bands, laid them on my desk, and walked out.

Our department was sorely short staffed, so I approached Ron and requested enough budget to add a second assistant. After the obligatory hesitation, he agreed. But who would be a good fit with Myles and me? Certainly not that Jon Corfino guy—the one who took over my corporate sponsorship job.

That's exactly who I hired. Jon was a friend, a back-stabbing friend, but a friend. But he was a good addition to our office. (Just kidding about the back-stabbing part.)

Ron left the decision to me as to whom I would hire, but he didn't think Corfino was the right choice. However, I had seen Jon's work ethic at Screen Test and felt he was the right person for the job. Ron would later come to agree that Jon was not only a good choice, but an excellent choice.

While at Screen Test a few years earlier, I met a young lady named Judy, visiting the park one day. She seemed very nice, very likeable, and very pretty. So I introduced her to Jon. He was a lonely, lonely person, and obviously needed my help. Hmmm. They hit it off right away and began dating, soon after got engaged, and then married. Today they have children and live just a few miles from me in southern California. I run into Judy occasionally at the local wholesale outlet. Jon, not so much. He won't even return my calls. Another hmmm.

With our entertainment department team assembled we needed a space that would accommodate us, because the office was so small there wasn't room for four desks, literally. Our total office space was a bit larger than two walk-in closets.

I explained to Ron the theory I mentioned earlier, that the size and location of an office speaks to the value placed on that department by corporate. I'm not sure he agreed with my philosophy, but gave permission for us to move. But, there was no available office space. What to do?

How about a trailer? Good idea. I was originally hired in a trailer-office. So we ordered a large trailer and waited for delivery. A few weeks later our new office arrived, and oh were we happy.

It came with a generous-sized lobby and reception area for Teresa, a fairly good-sized office for Myles, a very spacious office for me, including a sitting area for conferencing, but unfortunately an extremely tiny office for Jon. His office was barely big enough to accommodate a desk and a chair. Maybe that's why he no longer returns my calls. But we made the office work, and enjoyed the comfort of space. Now we needed to furnish it.

I was given a furniture budget and spent it wisely, until it came to buying a chair to go with my desk. I decided to splurge and get a really nice chair.

A week or two after the chair arrived, Ron showed up at the office. "I had to come see the chair," he said. Apparently, it became a topic of discussion on the hill. I knew it was expensive, but not so much that the general manager would make a special trip to check it out. Ron didn't have the same appreciation for the chair that I did, so I offered to return it, but he told me to keep it. It was a great chair, and for only $800 (today's value).

Great friends of mine, Dennis and Carol McBride, wanted to bring their son, Jamie, to the studio. "Of course. I'll meet you in the lobby Thursday morning and get you in." I wish I could blame this on being too busy, but the truth is, I just forgot they were coming. Dennis and Carol were some of Pam's and my dearest friends. They finally gave up and went home, after waiting in the lobby a looong time.

When I was reminded that I forgot them, I felt terrible. I called. "I'll make it up to you," I said. "Be ready at your house tomorrow at 10:00am." I didn't tell them what to expect, just to be ready.

I quickly got on the phone to Susan, a friend in the PR department, explained what I had done, or actually what I had *not* done, and asked if she could arrange a limo. So the next morning at 10:00am a limo pulled up in front of their house. I also sent one of my employees, Dan Rogala, along as the photographer of the day, to capture everything for them on camera.

An hour or so later they arrived in the passenger drop-off area just outside the tour entrance. I had also arranged for all of our strolling characters—Woody Woodpecker, Frankenstein, the Phantom, Baby Frankenstein—to greet them when they arrived.

The lobby was crowded with guests, and as the limo stopped, heads began turning to see what all the commotion was about, and what celebrities might be arriving.

With the costumed characters making a fuss over them as they stepped out, plus Dan hopping around like paparazzi, catching it all on camera, it made quite a spectacle for our guests. Many of them began snapping pictures of Dennis, Carol, and Jamie, even though they had no idea who they were—although I must say, Dennis is a celebrity in his own right. He has travelled the world as a master yo-yo champion.

We put them in the The Great Chase show as Wilbur and Maude at the Screen Test Theater. I stepped out of my entertainment director role and once again hosted/directed the show.

After the show we held a ceremony where I presented them with awards for Best Actress, Best Actor and Best Supporting Actor in the Completely Ridiculous Role category.

Carol passed away several years ago and Dennis married a wonderful lady named Linda. They live in Arizona, and yes, they're still very dear friends.

It was decided that the entertainment department needed a vice president. Rather than look inside the employee pool, someone was brought from the outside. Much to our surprise it was a person with no entertainment experience. As odd as it sounds, an attorney was hired to fill the position.

It wasn't that he and I had intentional conflict, but there always seemed to be underlying tension. Our personalities never gelled. Unfortunately, he knew nothing about entertainment, and fortunately, he didn't last long.

After his departure I asked Ron, "Do you see me advancing to that position?" To which he replied, "No. You're too nice a guy."

Was that a compliment? I wasn't sure. I knew my management style was different from Ron's, but okay, "I am where I am." Entertainment director was it. In a way I understood where he was coming from.

A few months earlier Ron had suggested that I fire, or at least move, a couple of people in my department. He didn't insist that I fire them, he just made the suggestion. Just a word of advice, when the boss suggests something, if it doesn't violate social or moral law, do it. I didn't.

In hindsight, he was right. Neither of them should have been where they were. But, because of my inaction with those two people, Ron saw me as unwilling to make the hard choices. He hadn't seen the other tough decisions I made as manager. But that was my fault. I was never comfortable making sure the boss saw everything I did. He paid me to run my department. So I ran my department.

I wasn't interested in parading my duties before him. For some people, "sucking up" is a way of life. I find the behavior disturbing.

Jay Stein considered the mark of a disciplined manager as someone willing to fire a friend. He did that with Cliff Walker. He and Cliff were good friends, but Jay fired him many years earlier. One of the people Ron wanted me to remove was a good friend, and the other was an office person. Hindsight ... sigh.

As is true with most people, I was always looking for ways to make things better. So ... "Why not film all of the shows in the entertainment center? It could be used for PR, or to sell as souvenirs. That's a good idea, Jerry," I thought to myself. Isn't it interesting how good we can make our ideas sound ... to ourselves. But when I presented it to management, they felt it was only a $5,000 idea.

Okay, what could I shoot with 5K? The answer, not much. What about the animal show? The actors were cheap. So I assembled a crew of four and over the next few days, using one camera, shot a fifteen-minute version of the animal show that looked like a multi-camera shoot. We even included a storyline about a mouse sneaking into the animal show to break into show biz. Now who wouldn't like that story? Fievel comes to Universal.

The crew of four included Joe Futerman as director of photography, a couple of techs, and me as director. My son Jonathan, five years old at the time, was our actor.

It's hard to imagine, but we ran out of money before completing the project. Five thousand dollars doesn't go as far as it used to. I don't think the studio ever used the video, but somewhere, in the archives at Universal, is our memorial to the animal show.

A friend introduced me to Billy Speer, a guy with an incredible voice, who wanted to produce a music video aimed at kids. After checking with the appropriate bosses, we spent a couple of days shooting what turned out to be a very cute rough cut of a pilot for the show.

Our video production included Billy (now "Cowboy" Billy) singing songs while interacting with kids around the park; marching down the bridge from the War Lord Tower, playing the comedic character in the stunt show, and battling the fire-breathing dragon in the Conan show. Keep in mind, Billy was not the average run-of-the-mill Conan superhero or stuntman. He was a robust fellow in excess of four-hundred pounds, but one of the kindest, gentlest, most jovial of people, and with a magnetic personality that everyone loved.

Although we lost touch for a while after finishing Cowboy Billy, we remained distant friends and finally reunited when I went to Orlando several years later to help open the studio there.

Billy passed away October 25, 2016, but his music lives on through his loving wife, Paula, and family. He was a great man!

The Parrot's Perch was another independent film project that we shot on the hill. The movie, based on a true story, centered on a man named Barry who was captured by the local authorities in Brazil and tortured using what is known as a parrot's perch.

We filmed a portion of the movie using sets at the A-Team show, which represented the perfect location of a border crossing in South America, plus other less-defined Brazilian locales.

After a couple of weeks shooting in various locations around the city, Barry said to me one day that he had to take an unexpected trip to Australia for a short time and would then return to complete the project. He took the dailies with him and never came back.

Funny thing, several years later when I was working in Orlando, Cowboy Billy called and asked if I wanted to get together for dinner with him ... and Barry, from the Parrot's Perch. I agreed. Barry never brought up his sudden need to go to Australia in the middle of our filming, and I decided to let it go. If he wasn't going to bring it up, neither would I.

There's an old saying that came to mind—if you loan someone twenty dollars and never see them again, it was probably worth it.

Did you ever do something that you just didn't want to talk about because it hurts too much? That's where I am in my story. But since this is my "twenty-five years inside Universal Studios," here goes.

The entertainment department was running smoothly. Myles was overseeing the shows and Jon had oversight of the strolling characters, show control personnel, KITT car, etc. In addition to overseeing the department I was toying with several side-projects outside Universal.

I called Ron one day and asked if we could meet for lunch. We met at Whomphoppers restaurant outside the tour lobby. After a brief conversation I told him I was going to leave the studio. He was surprised and told me, "I thought you were going to say that Jon or Myles was leaving."

Reliving that ordeal still hurts today. It was the greatest job in the world and I loved it, but somehow lost my focus. It was certainly one of the worst decisions of my life, maybe *the* worst.

After leaving Universal, I was without a job for a year while watching all my side projects fall by the wayside. I was looking to stay involved in the business, so a friend of mine, Paul Webb, asked me to produce a couple of promotional videos for the Union Rescue Mission in downtown Los Angeles. It was during my absence from Universal, so I was anxious to do it.

Paul has been in the business for many, many years. He has acquired a vast number of old movies and television shows numbering in the thousands, and as of this writing he is developing a movie classics cable channel, similar to AMC or Turner Classic Movies. Smart guy!

Around this time I heard from Terry Winnick, who was consulting for Old Tucson, just outside Tucson, Arizona. Old Tucson is a prime filming location where over four-hundred movies and commercials have been shot. The facility is open to the public and offers rides and a Wild West stunt demonstration.

In 1986 Terry called. He wanted to know if I was interested in consulting on their stunt demonstration. It needed a facelift. Because it was Terry, my answer was easy. Yes.

But I wasn't going to tackle the project alone. I needed someone who knew stunt shows. I called Lance. Together he and I went to Old Tucson and began evaluating the show. It lacked professionalism.

One of the most obvious problems was the lack of a theater, a stage, and seating for the audience. Guests stood along the sidewalks and in the street, anywhere there was available space. The actors did as much as they could with what they were given.

We made suggestions, recommendations, and wrote reports, but in the end the company that owned Old Tucson wasn't willing to put in the money needed.

Somehow the studio was continuing to function without me. Go figure. Actually, I was never under the assumption that I was a central figure in the grand scheme of things, but just a player in the wonderful theme park experience at Universal ... and I missed it ever so much. I missed the whole environment, but in particular hosting shows. I loved performing and interaction with the audiences.

In 1988 Universal decided to change the Screen Test show from The Great Chase to Star Trek. Phil Hettema, a man with an impressive résumé, was hired to produce the show. I had never met Phil.

The show's budget was significantly larger than anything Screen Test had ever seen, and Phil made the most of it. Very impressive! The show would feature the original cast from *Star Trek*, and of course incorporate guests from the audience. The same concept, just a different theme and bigger budget.

Since the early days of Stage 70, every new show carried over the same crew, Don, Bob, Larry, Joe, and me. But with the new show, all jobs were re-evaluated and everyone had to earn the position, especially the job as host/director.

After evaluations were done, Don was rehired as the technical director and Formica as one of the cameramen. This is the show when the budget was increased to include a second cameraman, and Joe and Larry were also hired as cameramen.

I heard about the auditions and showed up, along with about forty-plus other Hollywood hopefuls. Having previously hosted over thirty-thousand shows, or serving as director of entertainment, held no value. Bummer! So, get in line and wait my turn.

Auditions were held in a trailer on the lower lot and, yes, there was an actual line waiting to give it a try. I was somewhere toward the back.

I made it through the first round, but people were being cut every day. We were never sure who or when someone might be given the boot. The remaining pool of wanna-be show hosts was getting smaller. You were considered an optimist if you brought your lunch to work. Eventually, we moved the winnowing process to the park and onto the stage. Construction was still going on, so we had to work around that.

There is a truism I've found with every new show I've done. Perhaps it's just with me, I'm not sure. After opening a show, things go well for a couple of days, then suddenly there's a let down. There comes that inevitable day where my performance tanks, takes a nose dive, and, well … sucks.

Fortunately, after a show or two, things usually go back to normal. I think marathon runners call it "hitting the wall."

However, rather than waiting for the show to open and then hitting the wall, I tanked a couple of days after getting onto the set at Star Trek ... while the audition process was still underway. Guys and gals were still being cut. It came my turn one day and I went on stage, did my hosting/directing thing, but I hit the wall and my performance sucked. I was disappointed.

I've tried to be honest in telling my story, including the things that were hard to say—getting divorced, getting dumped by my girl friend, saying stupid things, making the dumb decision to leave Universal, etc. So in telling the next part of my story I'm communicating the words that were said, being careful not to embellish, but just tell what happened. I'm setting aside ego.

Just as I finished my less-than-stellar performance on stage, I saw Phil coming up from his place in the audience where he watched rehearsals. I wasn't sure if he was going to offer some corrective criticism, or give me the boot. I braced myself, expecting the worst. As he approached I said, "Sorry, I know that was pretty bad."

His response caught me off guard. He said, "Jerry, don't worry about it. You're in a totally different league than the others."

To say I was shocked would be an understatement. I was stunned. But as I reflected on his comment, I was also humbled.

Several days later in the rehearsal process, as opening day was drawing near, the bosses and their bosses were gathered in the back of the theater, discussing the show. I was in the distance, going through the show in my mind, and occasionally glancing in their direction as Phil was filling them in on the show's progress. I was too far away to hear what was being said, but suddenly all of them, in unison, turned and looked in my direction. I was embarrassed to be caught watching them. I wasn't sure what was being said, but soon after I was told that I was going to host the opening day festivities.

Everyone was so focused on opening day that everything else fell by the wayside. It was going to be the biggest opening Screen Test had every experienced.

The Star Trek budget included enclosing the theater. We were now a bona-fide indoor theater with huge screens for replaying our finished movie at the end of the show, rather than using those tiny little twenty-six-inch TVs spread out across the front of the theater.

Phil Hettema worked with his team and created magnificent sets.

Actors involved in the *Star Trek* TV show and movies were scheduled to attend, including Gene Roddenberry, William Shatner, George Takei, Nichelle Nichols, DeForest Kelley, James Doohan, and Walter Keonig. Everyone would be there except Leonard Nimoy. I heard something about him attending a Vulcan family reunion. (Vulcan humor, so it doesn't have to be funny.)

The press was there in full force. The theater was beyond packed, with every square inch of space occupied. Backstage was a beehive of activity. But interestingly enough, with the return of the same crew—Don as TD, Formica on camera one, Larry and/or Joe on camera two, a few other returning crew members, and me as the host—we were, for the most part, pretty laid back. This wasn't our first dance.

A new host/director, John Crane, was added to the rotation ... another good guy. We were always fortunate in finding good people to be part of the team.

John was an interesting choice as a host (in a good way). He and I were polar opposites in style. He was, and still is, about the same height as Al Gries. But where Al used calm and body language to his advantage on stage, John had a more frantic approach. He was the adrenalin-infused director hurrying all over the stage, here and there, pumping up the guests, keeping them and the audience involved and on edge (in a good way). I got tired just watching him. But his style worked very well for him.

John went on to write for television after the show closed. We ran into each other when attending Formica's funeral in Las Vegas a few years back.

Egos had to be checked at the door; otherwise, the crew would check it for you, especially Formica. If you were the show host, the guy with the microphone, big deal. Get over it. Try doing the show without the cameramen or TD. So we kept things in perspective, and although we no longer had blood lettings, we never had a problem with egos.

The celebrities began arriving. I said hello to Gene Roddenberry and we talked for a while backstage where I gave him the general rundown of what was going to happen. He, too, seemed laidback and relaxed. I greeted the other members of the original cast, then spent time talking with William Shatner. The idea was for him to serve as co-host with me as we did the first Star Trek Adventure at the Screen Test Theater.

"Let's get a microphone for Mr. Shatner," I said to one of the stage managers.

Then came a deer-in-the-headlights look. "We don't have one set up." Apparently, none of the techies had thought of having a microphone for the Celebrity of the Day!

A look of concern was transferred to me because I had done shows with a co-host, and it doesn't work with only one microphone. I couldn't stand in one place and direct the show; I had to move as the action moved and the scenes changed. For the audience to hear Shatner's comments, he would have to stay close and follow me around like a little puppy dog. Not a good idea. However, show time had come. We had no choice but to continue with one microphone.

The stage managers made sure everything was ready and everyone in place, then called for quiet.

"Ready, Jerry?" the stage manager asked.

I nodded. "Ready."

Universal had spent millions on this new Screen Test show, and Jay was banking on great publicity.

The curtains were closed so the audience couldn't see anything on stage. The house lights dimmed and rather than open with a great fanfare, the music faded as I stepped from behind the curtains. Flashes began going off all over the theater.

"Good afternoon, ladies and gentlemen, and welcome to the Screen Test Theater's Star Trek Adventure."

The media and audience wasn't there to hear a speech, so I cut to the chase and told them they were in for a real treat.

"Before we open the curtains and officially begin the show, I would like you to meet the gentleman who started the phenomenon on which our show is based. He is the producer, writer, and creator of Star Trek, ladies and gentlemen, please welcome (dramatic pause) ... Mr. Gene Roddenberry."

A thousand camera flashes before was now multiplied times twenty. We could have lit up Manhattan. The audience, filled with the media, invited guests, paying guests, and Trekkies, went crazy.

After what seemed like an eternity, the applause and cheering subsided and Roddenberry expressed his gratitude to Universal, and more importantly the fans. We chatted for a couple of minutes and then it was time to meet the other celebrities.

The plan was to briefly interview each celebrity and then they would stand on the side of the stage and observe for the duration of the show.

So one-by-one I called out each Star Trek star from the original cast. Finally, it was time for the big guy. "Ladies and gentlemen, please welcome Captain Kirk, commander of the Starship *Enterprise* (another dramatic pause) ... William Shatner."

Shatner came on stage and the house lit up like a Christmas tree, with thousands of camera flashes that continued for the rest of the show. We really didn't need stage lighting, because we had more than enough coming from the audience. Shatner and I chatted for a bit and then it was show time.

I thanked him and the other celebrities and ... "I think it's show time, Mr. Shatner. What do you think?"

"Yes it is," he agreed.

I turned to the audience. "Ladies and gentlemen, welcome to the Star Trek Adventure." And with that the Star Trek theme filled the theater and the curtains began to part. From upstage the full-sized bridge of the Starship *Enterprise* started moving slowly downstage toward the audience.

The set was an exact replica of everything fans had seen on TV and in theaters. It was really cool.

For the first scene I tried to stay close to Shatner, but he didn't know to move when I needed to move. I remember once asking him a question and when he took too long to respond I said, "Gotta go," and took off to get the scene finished. To be honest, I wasn't sure how the show producer, Phil, and management felt about me cutting off the Celebrity of the Day. But I had to keep the show moving. I didn't want it to drag. We needed to maintain a good rhythm.

I actually felt bad for Shatner. If he had a microphone, it would have been much better for him. He could make comments when he wanted and not feel left out. But it wasn't meant to be. His comments would have affected the show's timing, but we could have adjusted to it.

The show went well, and we ended close to the allotted time, which was a miracle for a debut. Not a miracle in the biblical sense, but we had never had a first show end even close to the correct time. That might have something to do with having several days of rehearsal prior to opening.

After the show, security worked hard to keep everyone off the stage except the media. But even with limited availability, the stage was flooded with reporters and camera crews, everyone seeking interviews with the Star Trek cast and Mr. Roddenberry. Only a few were interested in talking with the crew. We were not the news of the day.

Ron Bension made his way on stage after the show and worked through the crowd to find me. "Jerry, you're the best," he commented, followed with a pat on the shoulder.

After the euphoria of opening day, life settled in at Star Trek. With the initial hullabaloo over, shows developed a permanent rhythm and style. They take on a personality that is different from press day.

The first show always got lost in the glitz of the celebrities and media. With that behind us, John (the other host) and I began to make it our own—different styles, but both worked.

In addition to the bridge of the *Enterprise*, we had a set where we beamed away four people, just like in the TV show. But we did it in front of a live audience. One moment the actors were standing there in full view, then the glittery sparkles slowly replaced them and they were gone. The audience loved it. It drew applause and cheers every time.

The villains of the story were, of course, Klingons, those mean, vicious aliens intent on wreaking havoc on our poor innocent *Enterprise* crew. It was always comical to see guest actors trying to play the part of the evil Klingon leader.

One of the last scenes involved our guest actors battling a multi-legged creature that descended and hovered just over the stage floor. As always, the scenes shot on stage were edited with footage from the movie and our guest actors got to see themselves on screen with the Star Trek cast.

It was a popular show and my family paid regular visits. Both sons, Matthew and Jonathan, made it a point of being in as many performances as possible.

One of the most memorable, yet least effective uses of our time was when middle management decided we would be better show hosts/directors if we had acting lessons. The management team was relatively new and inexperienced and they reasoned that acting lessons was just what we needed to put us over the top. Never mind that our ratings were holding strong.

The Screen Test crew wanted me to go over the managers' heads and talk to Bension about it being a waste of time, but I had voluntarily given up my management job and returned to Universal as an employee. So it wasn't my position to go against what they wanted. They were in charge. Besides, management was paying this acting coach to do a job, and we didn't want to add undue hardship on him. He was doing what he was hired to do.

But hosting/directing is *not* acting. As a matter of fact, it's just the opposite.

The multi-day ordeal was comical, to say the least. The instructor had us hopping around the stage and doing all those things acting coaches do to "stretch" the actors to achieve character. Neither he, nor management, understood that the personality of the host/director *is* the character.

The day the acting classes ended was the day we forgot everything we were told by the acting coach. He was good as an acting coach, but probably never hosted anything in his life.

By February 1989 Terry had returned to work at Universal, and was heavily involved in plans for the theme park in Orlando, which by this time was moving forward at full speed.

A press conference to offer a sneak preview of the Florida park was scheduled for simultaneous broadcasts in New York and Orlando on February 28. Jay Stein was hoping that every press person in the world would attend.

One day Pam and I were having lunch at Black Angus in Burbank. Terry called. Actually, this was in the days before every man, woman, and child on the planet had a cell phone, so he paged me. I found a pay phone and called him. He said they wanted me to serve as master of ceremonies for the press announcement in New York. It was Terry asking, so it goes without saying, of course I would. The two events would be coordinated; Manhattan being the primary focus and Orlando supplementing.

The week arrived and I traveled to New York. Terry was already there. I checked into the hotel (everyone seemed to be staying in different locations). The next day we would meet at the venue where the press event was to be held. Upon arrival I found that preparation was already underway to make the room "theme park" ready. Artist renderings and scale models of the Orlando property were strategically placed.

I arrived at the theater in late afternoon. MCA/Universal top brass was there to be a part of the announcement. Steven Spielberg would also be part of the event. I thought of him as my back up. (Cue the laugh track.)

I knew ad-libbing for this event was not the order of the day. There was a script. So I spent time memorizing. The event would be typical in that I would open, then serve to provide segues between some of the guest speakers. There was no going off script, unless absolutely necessary.

For the most part I did stick to the script and ad-libbed only when delays in the event occurred. When hosting those types of events with little to no rehearsal, there are always unexpected challenges during the ceremony.

I can only imagine how excited Spielberg must have been when he heard he would be working with me. Hmmm. Maybe not. Actually, aside from an informal acknowledgement, he was always contained by a crowd of MCA big-wigs who occupied his time and attention. Both Wasserman and Sheinberg held Spielberg in the highest regard. Nothing was too good for him in their eyes, even to the point of giving him a percentage of the gross sales of Universal Studios Florida, for life. But frankly, with him Universal Studios Florida moves forward. Without him, probably not.

But the *event* was my focus, and my job was to make sure the transitions happened as they should. Lew Wasserman, Sid Sheinberg, Jay Stein, and Steven Spielberg were the true heavyweights in show biz–in all of show biz. Lew Wasserman was the CEO of MCA, and as I stated earlier, a legend and the last of the Hollywood moguls. Sid Sheinberg was the president of MCA. Jay Stein was president of MCA Recreation Services, and would later be inducted into the International Association of Amusement Parks and Attractions (IAAPA) Hall of Fame. Steven Spielberg was, well, Spielberg, the consummate wordsmith who could craft imaginative word pictures to sway any audience. They didn't need help to look good.

This wasn't going to be an opening night followed by multiple performances. It was one and done. And let's face ... if Wasserman, Sheinberg, Stein, or Spielberg messed up, so what. They owned the night. But if Jerry messed up, then it would be....

"Do you remember a guy named Jerry Green? He used to work at Universal Studios."

"No, not really."

"Didn't think so. No one does. He's the one who screwed up the Universal Florida press event in New York."

So there was a fair amount of pressure. I always tell people, butterflies in the stomach can be a good thing, as long as you get them flying in the same direction. If I was nervous at an opening or press event, I always tried to keep it hidden. Why let anyone know?

The magical day arrived. We met at the theater, and it was packed with every media variation imaginable. Fortunately, I can say the evening went off without a hitch. Jay received all the press he could possibly hope for. Wasserman, Sheinberg, and Spielberg were pleased.

Terry and I, along with some of the behind-the-scenes crew, went to dinner afterwards and reviewed the evening. There was no downside. If the bosses were pleased, Terry was pleased. Whew! (Although I must say, I'm seldom completely satisfied with my performance, and can usually pick out things I would do differently if given a second chance. Is that being a pessimist or a perfectionist?)

One of the requirements Wasserman and Sheinberg placed on Jay was to find a partner to share the cost of building the Florida park. If the Orlando park was such a good idea, it should be easy to find someone to put up half the money.

One of the first companies that Jay approached in July 1981 was Paramount Pictures. Who do you think was president of Paramount at that time? Michael Eisner. Jay presented his vision to Eisner, hoping to entice Paramount to join them. However, the plan backfired when soon after Eisner left Paramount to become president at … Disney. Yikes! And he took with him the knowledge of everything Universal intended for the new Florida venture.

After Eisner's arrival at Disney, it wasn't long before plans for the Disney-MGM Studios tour took root. In a race to get to the starting line first, Disney rushed to build their theme park and open before we did. So on May 1, 1989, Disney-MGM Studios opened.

After reading an article in *Orlando Magazine* where the vision for the Disney-MGM Studios was laid out, Jay was convinced that Eisner had stolen his ideas.

To prove his argument, Jay had an independent analysis done to compare Universal's original drawings and show concepts with Disney's plans. The general opinion, from those bold to assert their findings, backed Jay's claims.

(For an in-depth look into the struggle between Jay and Disney, I recommend the aforementioned *Jay Bangs*, from

Theme Park Press. It provides an insightful look at what Jay went through to bring his vision, his dream, to fruition, and contrasts the opening day shows and rides at Disney-MGM with those presented by Jay and the USF team.)

One of Jay's non-negotiables was that USF had to be a real working studio, not just a theme park. For twenty-five years, "going behind the scenes" was mentioned as *most important* in the exit polls at Universal Hollywood.

Although the studio wasn't ready for visitors at USF, in October 1988 the new Leave It to Beaver series began production in one of the sound stages in Orlando. Within the first year, thirteen feature films and five-hundred television episodes would go into production. Also in negotiation was a plan to bring all production for the Nickelodeon Channel to Universal Florida.

Dan Slusser, studio manger in Hollywood, was responsible for bringing much of the production to Orlando. Dan was a friendly, honest, and diplomatic man, and a big fan of the tour in Hollywood and Orlando. He became one of Jay's greatest allies.

On the other hand, Disney-MGM Studios struggled to attract production. In the mind of industry professionals and tourism, Disney was a theme park. Universal could wear both hats, production and theme park, and do it well.

An attorney friend of mine with a great sense of humor, who during his illustrious career argued before the Supreme Court, once said, "What do you call a hundred attorneys laying at the bottom of the ocean?" Then he would answer: "A good start." As much as we like to pile on when it comes to attorneys, not all deserve the watery grave. Universal had such a one, Tony Sauber. Tony was and is another one of the good guys. He spent twenty-six years as a key "problem solver" and strategist for Jay and MCA Recreation Services. Without Tony, Universal's road to the top would have been much bumpier. He had a special gift of making the complicated, simple.

Universal Studios Florida scale models

Universal Studios Florida scale models

As the war between Universal and Disney was going on behind the scenes, I went back to Hollywood and joined the planning and development team where our sister park on the other side of the country was the single focus. The P&D office was located off studio property, on the corner of Lankershim and Magnolia boulevards, in North Hollywood.

Finding corporate sponsors was the order of the day. A large room was devoted to scale models of rides and attractions for the Orlando park. My first assignment was to learn the corporate sponsorship spiel; how to describe each ride in a way that would entice corporations to sign on and have their name prominently displayed to our millions of visitors each year, but more importantly, to write a check to accompany that endorsement.

I recall listening for the first time to my counterpart explain the Jaws ride. He made the ride sound thrilling and scary.

Some Jaws enthusiasts may have taken issue with my earlier description that the "telling" of the Jaws ride was more frightening than the actual experience. But those who *experienced* both would probably agree with my assessment. Jaws was a fun ride, but came woefully short on the scare-meter.

After spending time learning the spiel, I never had a chance to use it. Terry pulled me from corporate sponsorship and had me focus on three other projects—a guided tour narration, a Screen Test Theater experience, and queue line entertainment for the E.T. ride. Later I would also consult on the Lagoon show.

The guided tour narration was a no-brainer because much of the narration from Hollywood would translate to Florida. And one advantage that Florida had over Hollywood was having Nickelodeon Channel in production most weekdays. Guests could see shows in production and often times be part of the audience, or even in a show.

I spent hours reliving my tour-guide days, and then more hours producing a rough draft of a tour narration. I would refine and finalize it when I went to Orlando. But production is production, whether in California or Florida, and was easy to incorporate in the narrative. And the jokes were bi-coastal.

Another project given me was to create queue-line-entertainment for the E.T. ride—trivia to take the guest's mind off the fact that they were waiting an hour-and-a-half for a three-minute ride. There were two queue lines for the ride, one exterior and one interior. And yes, guests got to experience both. My job was the exterior queue. The inside queue was Spielberg explaining the storyline of the ride.

I visited the research department on the lower lot and looked through photos and came up with questions. In the end, guests waiting to enter the theater were "entertained" while listening to filmmakers tell of their experiences on creating the film, and by answering trivia questions about Spielberg's mythical character.

When my part was completed I handed it over to the tech guys to incorporate into the queue.

Pam and I knew the Universal Florida project was going to be time-consuming and require sacrifice. But at first we didn't fully comprehend the extent of the commitment. We did know, however, that it was a great opportunity, and Universal was in my DNA. I had to go! Again, she was completely on board.

Our son, Matthew, was eleven, and Jonathan was five. She was home schooling them at the time, which she did for only one year, but that was the year. So there was never a break for her. The girls were already out of the house.

The job in Florida would last for over a year. My schedule was usually to spend two weeks in Orlando and then home for a long weekend, three or four days, maximum. Then repeat.

As I look back on that year, yes, it was challenging for the family, but I was thrilled to be involved in the USF project. Pam was thrilled also, but for a slightly different reason—she picked up my paycheck every two weeks from the studio.

For months I worked at Planning and Development in North Hollywood, prepping as much as possible so when the team moved to Florida we would hit the ground running. Barry Upson, the first general manager of the tour in the early days, returned to Universal and was now in charge of P&D. Peter Alexander, Bob Ward, and Terry Winnick, all VPs, were heading up the various projects.

Terry's assistant, "T," was a huge help in getting me oriented, keeping projects on track, and arranging travel for Terry and me to and from the East Coast. Her name was also Terry, so everyone called her "T," just to differentiate her from the boss.

I wasn't a workaholic but did spend my share of late nights and weekends working to keep my part of the projects moving forward. I remember one evening Terry and I were driving back over the Sepulveda Pass from an event in Santa Monica when he said to me, "I need some ideas for a new show."

I began rattling off some thoughts. After a few minutes he said, "No, not like that. Think bigger."

So I thought a minute then started with new ideas, bigger ideas. His face lit up and he said, "Yeah, I like that."

Although the project never received the green light, the ideas were used in a completely different show the following year that I wasn't a part of. But it didn't matter to me, I was happy to be a part of the process.

THE 1990s

A massive fire hit the back lot at Universal on November 6, 1990. It was deliberately started by a security guard with a cigarette lighter, who was hired to protect 21 "period cars" that were being used in the Sylvester Stallone film *Oscar*. The guard was sentenced to 4 years in prison in January 1992.

The fire destroyed a fifth of the standing sets on the back lot and total damage was estimated at around $50 million. It was started in Brownstone Street alley and the flames were fueled by gale-force winds and took hours to get under control. It was described as one of the largest fires in Los Angeles history and took 400 firefighters from 86 companies in LA and Burbank, along with 6 helicopters, to get it under control.

Sets that were damaged or destroyed included New York Street, Ben Hur, and Courthouse Square (used in the *Back to the Future* trilogy of films).

Everything that could be done on the West Coast was finished. It was time to head east. Terry was already in Orlando and settling into a new condominium he purchased.

I packed my bag, called the airport shuttle, kissed the family goodbye, and boarded the Delta flight to Orlando. Coach. VPs travelled in first, everyone else, coach. However, that would be my only time flying coach. Terry made sure of that. From then on I sat with the big guys.

One travel experience I always wanted, but I never had the opportunity, was flying on MCA's corporate jet. The closest I got was hearing Terry's description of it.

Interesting story about how MCA came to own a private corporate jet (as Terry explained it to me): the Wassermans were traveling on a commercial flight, and after the plane landed Mrs. Wasserman leaned over and whispered to her husband that that was her last flight unless he bought a private plane. No more commercial flights. Shortly after that, MCA became the owner of a private jet, and the Wassermans continued to travel together.

I arrived in Orlando and checked into the hotel. If I was going to live and work there for the better part of a year, why not stay in a nice hotel? The Peabody! A five-star hotel on International Drive. (The hotel is now the Hyatt Regency.) The view from my room atop the hotel provided a nightly display of the Disney World fireworks.

After being in Orlando for a couple of months, Pam and I decided she should come for a week's visit. She made the most of her time there. Each morning she dropped me off at the studio, then spent the day exploring Orlando in the rental car. She had a great time. After a week of R&R she returned home. I was alone again. Bummer.

Three months into my stay at the Peabody, accounting requested that I find a place with a weekly rate. My hotel bill in excess of $3,000 a month was impacting the budget. (Almost $6,000 in today's currency.)

The hotel, the luxury rental car, the great food—it was all wonderful, icing on the cake. But opening day was a reality, and now just months away. Everyone was scrambling, including me. I had projects to complete.

Nickelodeon was now a major player at USF, shooting most of their programs on the studio lot, so the tour narration had to be adjusted to accommodate them. We would provide great PR for them, and they would provide great PR for us.

A meeting was scheduled with the management team from Nickelodeon, including Geraldine Laybourne, executive vice president and general manager.

When she walked into the room, her first comment was, "I want to come meet the person who's hosted thirty-two-thousand live shows." I was surprised she knew.

Ms. Laybourne's only real concern was regarding thousands of guests constantly moving in and out while they were in production each day. But I assured her that we could make it work ... and of course we did. This wasn't our first rodeo. The USF and Nickelodeon relationship was always harmonious.

I come to understand the definition of "gak," and what it meant to be "slimed."

Screen Test shows, from the beginning, had always been performed on a stage in front of a live audience. Universal Florida was taking the concept in a different direction. Partnering with a company called Ultimatte, the show concept was replaced with an "experience."

Rather than a stage show, where only twenty to thirty people from the audience could participate, we chose a different scenario where anyone and everyone could be involved.

Forget the concept of a theater in the usual sense and think mini- soundstages, perhaps twenty feet in width. More like rooms, but mini-soundstages sounds more Hollywood. Each mini-soundstage was equipped with a green screen, a camera, and a show host. That's it! No set, no furniture. The sets and backgrounds would be on the green screen.

Terry was charged with oversight of the Screen Test Adventure. He hired a company to assemble a TV monitor-wall, and produce a video to explain the new Screen Test concept to our guests as they entered the theater lobby, and the options available to them. (The monitor-wall was made up of sixty-four TV monitors, eight across and eight high, and programmed together to function as one giant screen.)

Early on in the Screen Test project, the monitor-wall and video project were completed. The monitors were in place, the presentation cued up, and Terry asked me to come with him to take a look.

Upon entering the theater, the wall immediately grabbed everyone's attention. It was impressive and took up a considerable portion of the lobby. All sixty-four monitors synced together. Terry and I took a seat and sat back to watch the video presentation. As I recall, it was about five or six minutes in length.

The presentation was impressive, really impressive. Terry liked it. He congratulated the guys on a job well done, then asked if they would run it again. So we sat through a second showing. Then he requested a third showing. I was thinking to myself, "It hasn't changed since the last showing." But he's the boss, so we watched it again.

Then he asked, "How would it look if we moved this small scene closer to the beginning?" (I can't remember the specific scene.) The programmer accommodated his request and made the modification. Terry really liked what he saw, then asked if they could make another minor change.

After a couple of hours Terry had reworked the entire video, one small change at a time. As a result, the presentation flowed much better. I remember being so impressed with his diplomacy in getting the team who produced the video on board with his changes. And in the end they agreed it was better. Terry blended praise along with his suggestions, his requests. It was a pleasure watching the master at work.

The guest's screen test experience began when they entered the lobby and encountered the video wall. Two options were available. The first was to act in scenes from *Star Trek*, with the original cast. The beginning portion of the mini-movie included William Shatner and Leonard Nimoy interacting with the guests, on screen, giving acting advice. It was very clever.

A second option allowed the guests to re-create their day at Universal Florida, visiting the attractions and rides, and even included arriving at the studio in a limo. Both options provided an opportunity for the guests to experience their fifteen minutes of fame.

After selecting an experience, either Your Day at Universal Studios or The Star Trek Adventure, guests went to the counter and paid $29.95. They were assigned a director/host and escorted into a soundstage, and the "show" began. The new Screen Test concept provided far more souvenir sales because everyone who participated, bought.

Although the performances in each room were semi-private, it was still considered a show, and thus required a host. (Performances were semi-private because, although there was no audience, it was broadcast live on monitors in the lobby.)

However, from an operational perspective, filming in six mini-soundstages at the same time required in excess of thirty show hosts/directors to accommodate two shifts per day, plus breaks, and days off. My job was to find and train thirty people who could not just pull it off, but excel at it. The plan was to begin with a class of twenty. A training class larger than that would be unfair to the new recruits, because for most of them, it was their first attempt at hosting. From the group I also culled a few who demonstrated managerial skills to oversee the daily operation. A second class of hosts would follow once opening day was behind us.

To find the number of hosts/directors needed, we held auditions. Although our search was limited to existing USF employees, it was surprising how many showed up. I watched a lot of auditions over the course of two days. And although it was a constant parade of hopeful hosts, it's usually easy to spot those with the right skills.

I remember a few years earlier when I was entertainment director at Universal Hollywood. One morning while at a local coffee shop just down the hill from the studio, the restaurant manager asked one of my assistant managers if he could audition as a host for the A-Team show.

When I was told about the request, I thought, "Oh, really? Any professional experience?"

"Not really."

Hmmm!

Perhaps I felt sympathy for him, but for whatever reason we gave him a chance. We scheduled a time and a few days later he showed up on the set. I took a seat in the bleachers and nodded for him to begin. After about ten seconds I stood up, waved for him to stop. "You're hired," I told him. Obviously not everyone's talent is so evident. Some need prodding and grooming. But he had a natural charisma that wasn't being utilized as manager of the local coffee shop. (No offense to local coffee shop managers.) Several years later he became an announcer for a very popular network daytime game show.

It comes as no surprise, but nerves sometimes affect performance. I saw that a lot during the USF Screen Test auditions. When I sensed that was the case, I usually gave some coaching suggestions, and then a second chance. Everybody really wanted the job, but for a majority of them, it wasn't meant to be.

After hours of exhaustive auditions we had our team of show hosts, and for the next couple of days they memorized. I wanted them to be comfortable and confident with the words before we rehearsed. Later we would work on "playing the moment."

Universal Florida was like an ant hill. Hundreds of people, all busy with their own projects, scurrying to meet opening day. It was coming like a juggernaut.

Terry was focused on several projects referred to as "anchors." An anchor was one of the major rides or shows—Kongfrontation, Jaws, and Back to the Future. Before leaving California he had one of the original

DeLoreans from the movie shipped out via special
port to Orlando. The car had been sitting in storage for
a many years and I remember watching the driver racing
the engine, almost pedal to the floor, to get the car up
the ramp into the back of the truck. It had barely enough
power and we ended up helping by giving a push. The flux
capacitor wasn't fluxing.

To make opening day ceremonies special for the Back
to the Future—The Ride, the cast was invited to attend,
including Michael J. Fox, Mary Steenburgen, Tom Wilson,
and Christopher Lloyd. It was a spectacular event! As
themed music from the movie blared throughout the area
and smoke enveloped everyone, the celebrities arrived in
grand fashion aboard the train from *Back to the Future III*.
Yes, the train was brought in for that special occasion. As I
said, spectacular! (It always seemed to me as though Terry
failed to receive the credit he deserved for the success of
that ride. But that's probably my jaded view.)

Another anchor that was receiving attention, but not
in a good way, was the Jaws ride. Bruce the shark was not
being very cooperative. Spielberg named the notoriously
unreliable mechanical shark used in *Jaws* (the movie) after
his lawyer. I'm not sure if that's a compliment or not. But the
ride continued to be a thorn-in-the-flesh for years to come.

Even to describe the opening day ceremonies on June 7,
1990, as GARGANTUAN would be an understatement. It
was beyond that. The gathering of celebrities was stagger-
ing. US Airlines lent the studio a 737 to transport guest
stars like Jimmy Stewart, Ernest Borgnine, Anthony
Perkins, Sylvester Stallone, and Charlton Heston. And for
those stars who would never think of flying with common
folk, fifteen private jets were chartered.

However, once we got past the glitz and glamour, there
was the reality of operations. The celebs were there; the
guests were there. Gotta open the gates! To complicate

matters, it was hot—over 100-degrees, and rain! It's Orlando, of course it's gonna rain. It does almost every afternoon around 2:00.

To say that opening day didn't go well would be an understatement. Despite around-the-clock work during the final week prior to opening, many of the groundbreaking ride systems failed to function properly. And although the attractions opened, they continued to experience technical problems, closing frequently throughout the day. Some rides were being run manually by the tech crews behind the scenes. Men like Larry Lester, one of the go-to guys, was running full tilt to keep things functioning.

Larry Lester was the kind of person everyone wants on their team in crunch situations like we were in. He knew everything about everything—he was, in the fullest sense, a detail person. Ask Larry a question about how something works, then settle in because you're going to hear every minute detail. It wasn't unusual to see Jay Stein's eyes glaze over when Larry would tell too much. Jay just wanted to know why something wasn't working and when it would be up and running, not the history of a hex bolt and the material used to make it. But you knew if Larry was there, whatever was broken *would* be fixed.

As the day wore on guests were ready to storm the castle. We were handing out refunds, and later free tickets, to almost everyone. "Folks, we apologize. Here's a free ticket. Come back anytime for a visit."

Open, postpone, open, postpone? Was there really an option to postpone opening day? Not really. When an opening date is announced and guests invited, it's most disappointing to say to the world, "Just kidding. We actually meant forty days from now." We would have missed the summer season. Besides, if you wait for creative people to finish a project, opening day would never come. In their minds, there's always one more thing to tweak to make it better. (From a show host, and a writer's perspective,

I know that to be true. I wrote and rewrote my first novel, *Stealing Dawn,* at least forty times. If it wasn't already in print I could look at it today and want to make changes. But finally I said to the publisher, "I can't do it any more. It is what it is.")

We opened with twelve attractions including shows, rides, and two variations of guided tours. That was double the number Disney-MGM opened with (although three of our five anchor rides had issues that first day—Jaws, Earthquake, and Kongfrontation). After the first couple of hours, the Jaws ride got to the point where Tom Williams, park president, closed it down. Rumor has it that Spielberg got stuck on the ride for quite a while. (I was in a different area of the park and didn't see it, so that may be just a rumor.) But Jaws failed for several years to function the way it was designed. Before rushing to judgment, remember, we were pushing the limits of technology, and "going where no man has gone before."

Challenges, you bet. But we made adjustments, improvements, and took giant steps forward. Not only did we recover, but in our first year we out-performed Disney-MGM Studios, welcoming more than six million visitors. In surveys conducted by an independent company, eighty percent of our guests said they enjoyed Universal Florida more than they did Disney-MGM.

Although this may seem like an odd place to insert a comment about Ron Bension, it really isn't. He had a profound impact on both parks. I always thought of Ron as a good manager, but after seeing his influence in both Hollywood and Orlando, classifying him as a "good manager" comes up short. His managerial skills often turned disaster into gold, and he also had a creative side that played a huge part in visitors giving us that 80% approval rating over Disney-MGM. Hats off to Ron—manager extraordinaire. (He made only one blunder that I recall—he didn't make me VP of entertainment. Ron, Ron, Ron.)

As would be expected, we received criticism from the press for opening the park before its time. Jay even received some negative feedback from MCA management. But he believed in the old show-biz adage, the show must go on. He knew going in that there was a high probability of flaws on opening day, because P&D continued to tell him, "There's a high probability of flaws on opening day." But Jay knew, just as Disney had known, that our problems would be fixed and we would recover. He was 100% right.

When guests entered the front gate of Universal Studios Florida they stepped into the magical world of what most people *envision* Hollywood to be. Jay allowed no short cuts that compromised quality. It was, and remains today, a truly magnificent experience. Detail was the key. Jay insisted on it, and refused to allow anything short of authentic.

Every aspect of the studio was tied to a movie, television show, or craft. We wanted our guests to "Ride the Movies," a tag line Spielberg came up with a few years earlier. But more than that, Universal Hollywood had always provided our guests a behind-the-scenes experience into the wonderful world of movie-making. We told secrets known only to those in the industry. That same commitment would continue at Universal Florida.

With Opening Day behind us and the refining process in full swing, Terry assigned me another project. USF wanted to make a promotional movie, and because of his past relationship with Universal Hollywood, Robert Wagner seemed a logical choice for spokesperson.

Wagner, or RJ to those close to him, had been a friend of the tour from its infancy. He and Natalie Wood would often visit the park and were always friendly toward the guests. In addition to performing in over forty motion pictures, he starred in two television shows, *It Takes a Thief,* with co-star Fred Astaire from 1968–1970, and *Hart to Hart,* with co-star Stefanie Powers, from 1979–1985.

Since Terry was continuing to work on "fixing" other projects, he asked me to work as coordinating producer on the promotional video. We hired a company called ZM Productions, owned by Les Mayfield and George Zaloom. Les went on to direct movies including the remake of *Miracle on 34th Street*, with Richard Attenborough, and *Flubber*, starring Robin Williams.

We spent several days filming around the studio, and the ZM team did a good job. Of course RJ was a great sport. The movie promo saw him getting slimed on the Nickelodeon set (although his stunt-double took the gak); he was shot; knocked through a stained-glass window, falling two stories to the street below; almost run over by a crazed delivery truck driver; blown up by a ticking package; and finally, at the end of his horrific day, a demented limo driver dropped him for the night at his motel—the Bates Motel.

As my final weeks in Orlando were coming to a close, I completed the training of a second group of hosts for Screen Test, and also did minor consulting on the Dynamite Nights Stunt Spectacular, a show based on the TV series *Miami Vice*. It was a live stunt show that took place on the lagoon in the center of the park. The show featured pyrotechnics and explosions, jet skis and speed boats, but only performed after dark to enhance the pyro effects.

I missed being part of Universal Hollywood's opening by four years, but was ever-so-glad to be part of the Universal Florida debut. A shaky start? Absolutely. But Jay Stein, Ron Bension, Tom Williams, Barry Upson, Terry Winnick, Peter Alexander, Bob Ward, and the team at P&D (now called Universal Creative) took on Disney in a way no one thought possible. Where others tried and failed, Universal succeeded.

Jay started with an idea, that became a desire, developed into a concept, and then became a passion. Jay Stein took on Disney, and won.

One of the most treasured memories I have of those waning days at USF is Terry and I having lunch at Lombard's, one of several great restaurants in the park. We had a wonderful time discussing the ups and downs, the challenges and victories of the previous year, and even our years in Hollywood. We had experienced a lot together.

I returned to Hollywood, uncertain of what lay ahead. I had spent all but about one hundred days of the previous year in Orlando. Although my time there afforded me the opportunity to make frequent trips to Panama City to see my mom and sister, Linda, it was good to be home with Pam and the kids.

One of my first assignments back at USH was more training of show hosts. Several people were hired and assigned to me. The only challenge was that I hadn't seen them through the audition process. I soon found out that not all were meant to be show hosts. They had tour-guide skills, but not show-hosting skills. And as I said earlier, there's a difference. That isn't meant in any way to diminish the skills required for tour guiding. Show hosting is just different. Some who serve as tour guides can also host, but not necessarily everyone.

A few weeks after I arrived home Terry also came back. I don't remember how it came about, but he asked me to write some comedic material to run on an audio loop in one of the restaurants going into City Walk. Even to this day I cringe when I think about it because what I came up with wasn't good, and I knew it. And I'm sure Terry knew it also, but he never said anything.

I have been fortunate in my life to meet some of the most famous people in the world. I've interacted with them, shared ideas, planned events, and from time to time just sat and chatted about life in general. But one day Ron Bension made me an offer I couldn't refuse. Actually, now that I think of it, I never refused any offer Universal made. But this one was big!

I was asked to be part of a team from Universal to work with the Ronald Reagan Presidential Library dedication ceremony. You may ask, "Why would Universal Studios be part of the presidential library/museum ceremony?" No, it wasn't because President Reagan was Ronald Reagan the actor, prior to politics. Lew Wasserman, CEO of MCA, parent company of Universal, was a contributor to Reagan's presidency. Of course Universal also contributed to many other campaigns, Democratic and Republican. That's just the way big business works.

But our responsibilities on that momentous day would include working with the president's team on a couple of fronts. One was to provide trams. The library's small parking lot atop the hill in Simi Valley, California, would be turned into a seating area for several hundred guests and celebrities. Therefore, parking would have to be off site. Wasserman volunteered our trams to shuttle guests back and forth from the parking lot a mile away. That assignment fell to Felix Mussenden and Mike Taylor, operations managers. As mentioned earlier, Felix would later go on to run the studio in Florida and Mike the Hollywood studio.

My job was to help coordinate the docents. Although I must say, there wasn't much required on my part. The library supervisorial staff was excellent. A few operational meetings were required, as well as background checks on all of us by the Secret Service. I had my first use of a cell phone at the library. A Secret Service agent offered to lend me his phone so I could call Pam and tell her where I was and what I was doing. "Hey, sweetheart, guess where I am and what I'm doing?" The whole experience was very cool.

The event, held on November 4, 1991, was a combination of Hollywood and Washington D.C. celebrities.

I was given three tickets to the event so Pam attended with her parents. I thought this might be the thing that finally made her dad like me. But maybe not. (We really did like each other.)

The Simi Valley hilltop was swarming with elites, lesser elites, media, and Secret Service. There were even snipers on the surrounding hill tops. It was probably the most protected place in the world that day. It was exciting, and we were about to witness an event that was historical by any definition. It was show time....

A hush fell over the audience. "America the Beautiful" began playing softly in the background and the announcer started with introductions. As six First Ladies—Nancy Reagan, Pat Nixon, Betty Ford, Rosalynn Carter, Barbara Bush, and Lady Bird Johnson—approached the stage the music grew louder and hair began to stand on the backs of everyone's neck, while goose bumps tickled the skin. The

First Ladies walked up the ramp and stood center-stage, shoulder-to-shoulder, smiling and waving.

Then, after a time of applause ... attention was drawn to the courtyard.

"Hail to the Chief" filled the air and, for the first time in American history, five U.S. presidents began walking side-by-side through the colonnade, past the massive steel gates, up the ramp and onto the stage. Presidents George H. W. Bush, Ronald Reagan, Jimmy Carter, Gerald Ford, and Richard Nixon stood five abreast. Applause! Applause! Excited? Of course. But a more refined and dignified reception that one might expect at a Kanye West or Taylor Swift concert.

As the applause reached a crescendo, the men took their seats and Charlton Heston came to the podium. His speech, delivered as a prologue, should be required listening for every American, and those wanting to be Americans. He was followed by General Colin Powell who led us in the Pledge of Allegiance.

Next was the Color Guard marching to the front of the stage as the U.S. Army Chorus began singing the national anthem. I would say the goose bumps returned, but truth is, they never went away. Applause and appreciation were the order of the day.

Governor Pete Wilson of California served as host of the event. (Didn't they know I did that kind of thing for a living? Somebody didn't get the memo!)

Just a couple of weeks after the dedication, our team from Universal was invited to visit with President Reagan at his West Coast office in Century City. He was most gracious and kind, and expressed his appreciation for our part in making the dedication ceremony a success. Although the meeting didn't last long, it was indelibly imprinted in our minds.

I did a plethora of jobs in Planning and Development after returning from Orlando. But after a year, in early 1993, my career at Universal Studios came to an end.

Shortly after that I was hired as president of a production company in Vancouver, Canada, for a year. Our primary function was to make eight-minute infomercials for various companies. We put three mini-infomercials together to make a half-hour show. The project was interesting because one of the primary investors was the grandson of the last emperor of China.

By 1992 Terry had left the studio and gone to work for Circus Circus Casino in Las Vegas. Not too long after that he called. They were considering putting in a modified stunt show upstairs in the casino. He asked if I was interested in consulting. Of course.

I called Lance. Together we flew to Vegas and spent time considering all aspects of the venue they were hoping to use. In the end it wasn't remotely feasible unless they were willing to redesign the entire area. They wanted to turn something never intended as a theater, into a theater. Their stage was elevated about fifteen feet higher than the audience. To fix that alone would require major reconstruction of the entire theater.

After hearing of the costs associated with their idea, they decided to scrap the project. As much as I would have enjoyed putting in a show, it was the right decision to make.

In addition to Circus Circus, Terry also worked for Grand Casinos and designed more than 30,000 hotel rooms and 15 major casino properties in 7 states. He worked for Vale Resorts; he also worked with his son Zak during this time. (Many years later, in 2011, he started a charity called Postively Kids.)

A year or so after returning from Canada and finishing up work for Terry, two dear friends, David and Suzanne Johns, asked Pam and me to join them in a business totally unrelated to entertainment. That was a wonderful blessing for another twenty years.

IT'S A WRAP

I have to tell of one final meeting. Several seemingly unrelated elements make this story one of the most special in my life.

After Circus Circus, Terry and I didn't see each other for many years. Pam and I decided we would treat each of our four kids (and their families) to a trip, anywhere they wanted.

Matthew and Jonathan, being theme park enthusiasts, chose Orlando. No big surprise there. So Jonathan, Matthew, his wife Natalie and their three kids, Katelyn (Katie Mae to me), Ethan, and William, took off for several days to the Sunshine State. Hot and humid, but a great family time.

Our oldest daughter, Suzi, chose Hawaii. She and her youngest son Coby, Pam, and I went to Oahu. Yes, warm, but Hawaii is Hawaii. How bad can it be?

Our second oldest daughter, Kimi, had a life-long dream of going to New York. In November 2013, she, her husband Phil, and daughter Alexia (Lexi to everyone) packed up and took off for Manhattan. It was cold! Not Winnipeg cold, but cold. We did all the touristy things and had a great time.

One evening we went to see the Rockettes at Radio City Music Hall, my favorite Christmas show ever. After the show we decided to find a place to have dinner and began strolling along Sixth Avenue. Then after several blocks we randomly selected one out of a bazillion restaurants in Manhattan, and walked in.

I put our name on the reservation list and found that we had to wait only a few minutes. While standing in the lobby chatting I looked just ten feet from me and there stood .... Terry Winnick! I did a double-take just to make sure, then took a couple of steps toward him and asked ... "Terry?" I didn't want for some New York mafia guy to turn on me if I had the wrong person.

He looked at me and said, "Jerry!" His eyes lit up. To say it was a glorious reunion would be to state the obvious. His hotel was across the street and he had just walked over for dinner. We invited him to join us, then spent the entire evening talking, catching up, and reminiscing about the good ol' days. It was one of the most special evenings of my life. While sitting there he called his ex, Barri (they remained good friends through the years), so I could say hi. She and I were tour guides together.

I trust I'm not hurting anyone's feelings, but when Pam and I had lunch with Terry's friend Merrilee a year or so later, she told us that Terry talked about our Manhattan meeting for three days. As I mentioned earlier in my story, Terry and I had a "brother" relationship, much like that of Jerry Hood and me.

Over the following months Terry and I talked a couple of times on the phone and agreed that he and Barri, Pam, and I would get together for dinner on his next trip to southern California. We had done that from time to time when we were younger.

My son Jonathan also interviewed Terry via telephone regarding his days at the studio for a podcast on his website Inside Universal. Terry had a vivid memory and could rattle off dates and details with amazing accuracy. Things I had completely forgotten, or had the wrong dates assigned to.

Unfortunately, we never had the opportunity for our second reunion as Terry was diagnosed with cancer and passed away in November 2014. Barri asked me to speak at his funeral, for which I am eternally grateful.

Some may consider Terry and me "accidentally" running into each other in Manhattan as lucky. I disagree. First of all, there's no such thing as luck. There *is* providence. I am confident the Lord, being the God of mercy and blessing, orchestrated the meeting to give us one more opportunity to reconnect ... and it was a blessing. Just as a few years ago I was also able to reconnect with my childhood best friend, Jerry Hood, who still lives in Panama City. Believe it or not, God does care about the details.

As I said at the beginning of my story, for twenty-five years I was employed by the biggest and busiest studio in the world to design, write, direct, and perform in front of audiences *whom* I loved—over 32,000 times, over 1,280,000 minutes on stage—doing *what* I loved. For twenty-five years I *played for a living.*

IT WAS AN AMAZING RIDE!

ABOUT THE AUTHOR

Write an autobiography? I never considered it, until two of my kids suggested, then encouraged me to take the plunge. And the interesting thing is, my life boils down to one-hundred-fifty pages. It seemed longer.

Some people are born gifted writers. Others, not so much. I'm now finishing my third book. Yet when people ask me if I'm a writer, I always tell them, "I enjoy writing, but I don't know if I consider myself *a writer.*"

So what led me to write my first novel, *Stealing Dawn*?

At the age of 26 I became a Christian, and knowing the entertainment industry as a whole lacked moral character, I wanted to develop material that my wife and four kids could read, watch on TV, or see in the theater. From that desire came the idea for *Stealing Dawn*, an action/adventure story.

Originally written as a movie script, it sat in the closet for years before I decided to find out ... could I write a novel? Who knows, perhaps someday *Stealing Dawn* might make it to the big screen. There's the old saying, "Hope springs eternal."

My wife, Pamela, and I live in southern California and are blessed with four children, seven grandchildren, and now one great-grandchild. Perhaps I'm not as young as I thought!

For more, visit my website: jerrylanegreen.com.

More Books from Theme Park Press

Theme Park Press is the largest independent publisher of Disney, Disney-related, and general interest theme park books in the world, with over 100 new releases each year.

We're always looking for new talent.

For a complete catalog, including book descriptions and excerpts, please visit:

ThemeParkPress.com

Jay Stein Builds a Better Mousetrap

After years of sitting fat and happy atop the theme park totem pole, Mickey Mouse discovered a big cat in his backyard named Jay Stein. Against stiff odds, corporate politics, and fierce opposition from Michael Eisner's Disney, Jay Stein founded Universal Studios Florida.

themeparkpress.com/books/jaybangs.htm

Learn from the Disney Imagineers

Creativity. Innovation. Success. That's Disney Imagineering. It was the Imagineers who brought Walt Disney's dreams to life. Now *you* can tap into the principles of Imagineering to make *your* personal and professional dreams come true.

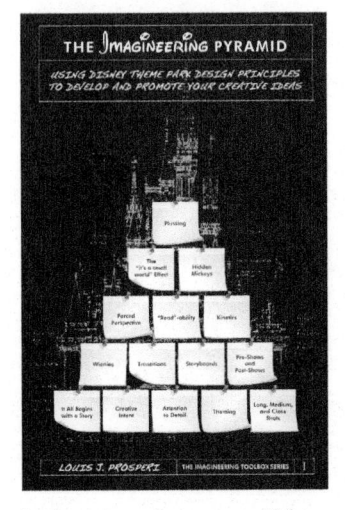

themeparkpress.com/books/imagineering-pyramid.htm

Walt Disney and the Pursuit of Progress

Think "Walt Disney" and you come up with animation and theme parks and Mickey Mouse. But Walt's real passion was technology. Documentary filmmaker Christian Moran (along with Rolly Crump, Bob Gurr, and others) provides a fascinating history of how Walt shaped the future while entertaining the masses.

themeparkpress.com/books/great-big-beautiful-tomorrow.htm

A Web of Disney

In this unique comparative history, newspaper journalist Chuck Schmidt traces the slender, often invisible strands that connect four monumental achievements in our pop culture: Disneyland, Freedomland, the 1964-65 New York World's Fair, and Walt Disney World.

themeparkpress.com/books/disney-dream-weavers.htm

The Imagineering Graveyard

On an alternate earth, Walt Disney World guests are taking in the thrills of Thunder Mesa, braving the Beastly Kingdom, marveling at Villains Mountain, and staying the night at Disney's Persian Resort. Want to join them? This is your guidebook to the theme park that Disney never built.

themeparkpress.com/books/walt-disney-world-never-was.htm

Welcome, Foolish Readers

Join your new Ghost Host, Jeff Baham, as he recounts the colorful, chilling history of the Haunted Mansion and pulls back the shroud on its darkest secrets in this definitive book about Disney's most ghoulish attraction. With exclusive photos and Imagineer commentary; updated for 2017.

themeparkpress.com/books/haunted-mansion.htm

Printed in Great Britain
by Amazon